Jennifer Lee

Master Your Emotions

Master Your Emotions

The Complete Guide to Know How are Destructive Emotions Made, Control your Anger, Relieve Stress and finally Rediscovering Positive Thinking

Jennifer Lee

Table of Contents

Introduction

Welcome to *Master Your Emotions*, a book dedicated to helping you swim strongly in the constantly shifting seas of human emotion. If you have ever felt crippled by fear, conquered by rage, torn by jealousy, or buried by depression, then you already understand just how destructive mismanaged emotions can be, and just how difficult it is to do the managing.

I have fought these currents, struggling for four years before learning how to master my emotional self. I am offering this book as a lifeline to anyone who has suffered as I have. I have filled these pages with tested and true techniques and strategies to identify, understand, and master your emotions. These concepts and tools have saved me from my lowest point, and I hope they do the same for you.

By choosing to pick up this book, you have entered into a contract with yourself, a commitment to understand and gain mastery over your emotional turmoil. I applaud you. To make this commitment is not an easy feat. It can often become comfortable to remain stuck in cycles of fear or panic or exhaustion because as painful and damaging as these reactions and behaviors are, they are familiar. To become a master of your emotions, you must commit to the task, leave the lifeboat that has kept you afloat, and face the raging water. Don't worry. I am here to guide you and help you swim by presenting all that I have learned over the course of my personal journey.

Understand that there are no quick fixes when it comes to emotion. Baby step by baby step—that's the only way to move forward, and the first step toward mastering your emotions is identifying and understanding what you are feeling and why. Are you ready to jump in?

Chapter 1: Identify and Understand Your Emotions

"Feelings are something you have; not something you are."
— Shannon L. Alder

It can often be too easy to let emotional health fall through the cracks as we weave through our hectic and complicated lives, letting negative feelings run rampant while we count every second of that rare moment of contentment. Or perhaps, you're less concerned with feeling happy than you are with feeling anything at all after years of suppressing your emotions, consciously hiding how you feel. Wherever your emotional distress comes from, understand that emotions make us human, but they do not define who we are.

It is okay to be confused or overwhelmed by your emotions; you are *not* immature, *not* weak, and *not* stupid for experiencing emotional turmoil. All too often, we see our emotional turmoil as a sign of inadequacy, but you are not inadequate, and you are not alone. We all have our own personal emotional struggles, and anyone can become lost in the storms they create. Understand that we're all confused, sometimes. What matters is that you're trying, and if you're reading this book, you already are.

Even scientists, psychologists, and professionals in the study of thoughts and emotion struggle to define and understand emotions because they are so difficult to observe and measure. Every individual's emotions are subjective to his or her own experiences, beliefs, thoughts, and reactions, and everyone interacts with the world in different ways.

What's more, emotions rarely manifest as single, distinct feelings. Instead, they oftentimes present simultaneously or one as the result of another, forming a confusing conglomeration of several emotions that language fails to express. This quotation from Jeffrey Eugenides's novel *Middlesex* explains this with uncanny clarity:

> "I'd like to have at my disposal complicated hybrid emotions, Germanic train-car constructions like, say, 'the happiness that attends disaster.' Or: 'the disappointment of sleeping with one's fantasy.' I'd like to show how 'intimations of mortality brought on by aging family members' connects with 'the hatred of mirrors that begins in middle age.' I'd like to have a word for 'the sadness inspired by failing restaurants' as well as for 'the excitement of getting a room with a minibar.' I've never had the right words to describe my life, and now that I've entered my story, I need them more than ever."
> — *Jeffrey Eugenides*

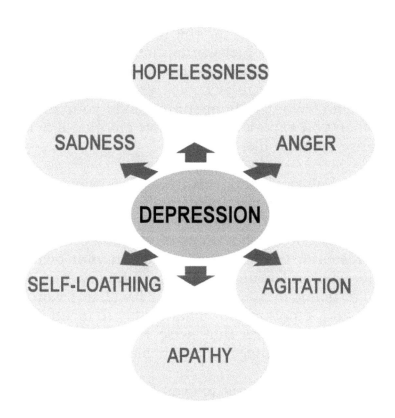

Your emotional self is a complex being, but there is no one better suited to understanding your emotions than you are. You can begin to overcome intense negative emotions by learning to recognize and understand what you are feeling and why.

What Are Emotions?

If I asked you to create a list of emotions, that would be easy, right? There's joy, amusement, awe, sadness, grief, anger, jealousy, fear, shame, and on and on you could go.

There are many names for the feelings you experience, but these names are just words, nominatives that fail to fully represent the complicated and subjective sensations you deal with on a regular basis. What, exactly, do these words mean? What is happening inside your mind and body when you experience a positive emotion like love or a negative emotion like anxiety?

Even psychological and scientific professionals debate the definition of emotion, some making clear distinctions between "emotion" and "feeling" and "mood" while others focus on the chemical sources of emotions. I encourage you to research these methodologies on your own if you are interested in learning more about theory, but for this book, I'm going to keep it simple. I will use words like "feeling" and "emotion" interchangeably to mean the raw, indefinable sensations that arise from inside, affecting our thoughts, responses, and behaviors.

All too often, it is difficult to even name the feeling being experienced, making emotional distress all the more intense. Perhaps, this list of simple definitions and some common symptoms will help you identify some of your own negative emotions.

- Fear/Panic - A response to perceived danger, physical or emotional

  o Perspiration

  o Cold sensations

  o Dizziness

  o Hyperventilation

  o Increased heart and breath rates

- Anxiety/Worry - Apprehension, pessimism, or a general sense of unease
  - o Stomach and/or chest pain
  - o Muscle tension and/or pain
  - o Changes in appetite
  - o Changes in sleep quality
- Anger/Rage - A hostile response to a perceived offense; irritability
  - o Increased heart and breath rates
  - o Surge of adrenaline
  - o Decreased ability to think clearly
  - o Lack of self-restraint
  - o Explosive outbursts
- Irritability - General state of aggravation, frustration; prone to anger
  - o Becoming easily upset/angry
  - o Increased heart rate
  - o Confusion and/or aggression
- Agitation - General state of irritability; inability to calm thoughts or sit still
  - o Racing thoughts
  - o Muscle tension and/or pain

- o Easily becoming upset

- Jealousy - Insecurity over perceived lack of something

  - o Sense of low self-esteem/self-worth

  - o Feelings of inferiority

  - o Feelings of resentment

- Sadness/Greif - A condition of despair, perceived disadvantage, loss

  - o Urge to cry

  - o Sense of helplessness

  - o Fatigue/lethargy

  - o Feelings of loneliness

- Depression - Severe sensations of despondency and/or sadness

  - o A generally depressed mood/state of being

  - o Feeling worthless or helpless

  - o Loss of interest, energy, focus, and/or pleasure

  - o Increase or decrease in appetite

  - o Thoughts of death or suicide

- Apathy - Indifference, lack of feeling

  - o Loss of interest

  - o Loss of concern

  - o Feelings of being without purpose

- o Fatigue/sluggishness
- Fatigue/Lethargy - Lack of energy, weariness, decreased motivation
  - o Feelings of boredom
  - o Feelings of being overly "stressed out"
  - o Lacking the incentive to be productive
- Guilt - Realizing or believing one has violated his or her own moral code; remorse
  - o Feelings of confliction over action or inaction
  - o Rumination on action or inaction
  - o Compulsive thoughts and behaviors aimed at repayment
- Shame - Humiliation; feeling of being improper or foolish
  - o Feeling inadequate while others "are perfect"
  - o Concealing feelings of low self-worth
- Self-Loathing - Low self-worth; believing one can do nothing right
  - o Criticizing oneself for perceived faults and flaws
  - o Rumination on past mistakes
- Doubt - Lack of certainty; delaying action due to indecision

o   Distrust in certain information

o   Lack of confidence in own abilities

o   Feelings of pessimism

- Timidity - Uneasiness; lack of self-confidence; awk-wardness

    o   Feelings of social anxiety

    o   Low self-esteem/self-confidence

    o   Crippling apprehension

Unfortunately, these definitions are limited because words, themselves, are limited. Trying to explain emotion is like trying to scoop up honey with a net. The honey sticks to the web itself, but most of the real substance slip through the holes. The best you can do is to try to understand your own emotions on a personal level. There are two main methods for understanding emotions: psychologically and physiologically. Both your thoughts (conscious and unconscious) and your body contribute to how you feel.

Emotions and Your Body

Emotion is not just a psychological affair. When you react to internal or external stimuli, there are changes in your body, such as elevated heart rate, increased blood pressure, perspiration, or the release of a specific chemical, which can significantly affect how you feel.

For example, when you are overly stressed, your body has a "fight or flight" response. A surge of adrenalin is produced by the body to prepare you to either face the situation or flee the situation, causing increased blood pressure, paling or flushing of the face, accelerated breathing, and other physical symptoms. If you've ever experienced an anxiety attack or panic attack, then you know how connected the mind and body are when it comes to emotions.

It's not only negative emotions that are linked to changes within the body. Many positive feelings are associated with certain neurotransmitters and "feel-good" chemicals. For example, a strenuous activity causes an increase in endorphin production, a hormone that reduces pain. Laughter also releases endorphins in the body as well as boosting immunity, decreasing stress hormones, and improving circulation and cardiovascular function.

Of course, physical symptoms of emotion are not always good or bad. There are some emotional symptoms that you may experience in both positive and negative circumstances. Increased heart rate and perspiration, for example, can indicate anger, but they can also indicate excitement or love.

Emotions and Your Mind

Your mind is unique. There is no other psychological framework like yours, and you will experience emotions differently than anyone else. Take falling in love as an example.

This may feel like weightlessness/lightness, or it may feel as if a million bees are trapped inside your stomach. It may be intense, or it may be subtle. It may be instantaneous, or it may emerge gradually. It is the same with anger, frustration, weariness, and even happiness. Just because you may not experience the same emotion in the same way as another person does not devalue what you are experiencing.

Because no two people will experience the same emotion in the same way, there is no definition that will be appropriate for every person. For example, two people battling depression may experience very different symptoms. The first may have trouble sleeping, have no appetite, and have no interest in things that were once enjoyable while the second has trouble with sleeping in too long, binge-eating, and intense waves of despair. These two instances of depression will look strikingly different from an external viewer, but both of these sufferers' emotions and experiences are valid and could be identified as depression.

This is why intense emotions like grief affect different people in such disparate ways. Two siblings facing the loss of a parent, for example, will each deal with it in his or her own way. The first may cling to family and friends for support in coping with the intense grief, while the other may become the family comic, cracking jokes to keep everyone smiling while dealing with the sadness in private. Neither of these responses is wrong; they're just different.

The trick is to stop comparing your emotional self to the emotional selves of others. Identifying and defining emotions in oneself must be a personal affair. When we compare ourselves with others, we end up invalidating our own feelings because they don't seem to "match what everyone else is feeling." Your emotions are yours, and they are valid already in the fact that you are experiencing them.

Understand Your Emotions by Sharing

"I am master of my spoken words and slave to those which remain unspoken."
— Ankita Singhal

One excellent way to better understand what you are feeling and where these emotions are coming from is to talk it out with someone you trust, even if that means you're sharing only with the blank pages in your journal. Try to describe what you're feeling. If it's anxiety that you struggle with, you may describe racing and unfocused thoughts, a hollow pit in your belly that persists for days, or an inability to sit still. If you suffer from depression, you may describe not being able to feel anything at all, known as apathy, or you may describe an intense and unrelenting sadness that makes you constantly want to cry. If you're overly stressed, you may describe feeling overwhelmed, or you may describe an inability to focus.

Whatever it is you're feeling, try your best to put it into words. The more you practice describing and expressing how you feel, the better you will understand your emotional self.

Try to give definitions to your feelings, even if there is no one word or phrase to describe it. Make a word up, or focus more on sounds than making sense, and say/write whatever rings true for you. If you can't articulate what you're feeling any more clearly than by letting out a guttural wail, then do it. Scream, cry, and wail— it doesn't matter so long are you are expressing yourself. Even if your name for your emotion only makes sense to you, being able to define it will give you power over it, and the more you practice expressing what you're feeling, the easier it will become. As you make your way through the rest of this book, you will learn how to cope with this complex and overpowering emotions, but the first step is identifying them.

Remember, emotions are a normal part of how we interact with ourselves and the circumstances and people who surround us. Having feelings is what makes you a human being. The problems start when emotions become destructive to our daily lives and our overall happiness.

Chapter 2: Know the Difference between Constructive and Destructive Emotion

"Anger can be a useful emotion; it's built into our genetic code to help with self-preservation. But it can also be destructive, even when it is justified."
— Michael Hayden

Emotions themselves are a natural part of how we interact with ourselves and with the world around us. We are designed to feel, to love and grieve, to find joy in our successes and disappointment in our failures, to worry, and to hope. Without emotion, we would be detached, robotic automatons wandering around without purpose. It is in the mismanagement of emotion that we become slaves to destructive cycles of feeling, which sap us of energy and motivation and cause us to have warped perceptions of ourselves. To master your emotions, you must be able to tell the difference between constructive emotion, which is helpful and useful and destructive emotion, which distracts, multiplies, and overwhelms.

Many emotions have the capacity to become destructive but are, at the core, constructive. Consider fear. When allowed to coalesce into itself, fear can become paralyzing, but fear itself is a natural defense mechanism designed to alert you to a perceived danger. The fear response is your brain telling your body that something isn't right. Fear is a part of your instincts, and you've always been told to trust your instincts. So, what happens? Where exactly is the line between constructive emotion and destructive emotion?

The line exists where emotion stops being help in navigating through life and becomes a hindrance. In other words, emotions become destructive when they cause the development of long-term barriers to your personal goals and happiness. For example, grief is a natural response when someone close to you passes away, but unchecked, overwhelming grief can be mentally and physically debilitating, keeping you from moving forward.

For most, emotions become destructive for one of two reasons. (1) The emotion is so intense that it overwhelms mindfulness and logic, or (2) the emotion is suppressed or repressed, which means it is being consciously or subconsciously avoided. Let's look at these two common sources of destructive emotion.

Destructive Emotion Is High-Intensity Emotion

We do not experience every emotion at the same intensity every time, by which I mean emotional intensity varies depending on what the experience is.

For example, you may experience a low-intensity grief after hearing the news that a favorite performer has passed away, but you may experience a much fuller, more intense grief at the loss of a friend or relative.

As low- and mild-intensity emotions tend to be easier to cope with, these are often constructive. You may cry over the loss of that beloved celebrity, but these tears would likely be cathartic, granting inner relief through the expression of the emotion. A high-intensity emotion, on the other hand, can be more difficult to face or cope with, causing emotional and psychological distress. The loss of a friend, for example, may cause much higher intensity of grief, making it difficult to continue with daily life.

Not everyone experiences emotions with the same intensity. Some of us are just designed to feel more intensely than others. If you've ever found yourself overcome with emotion over what was, for others, a mundane situation, then you may be an intense feeler. This is not a bad thing, because it also means you feel positive emotions more intensely, but being an intense feeler may be why you struggle with mismanaged emotions. The higher the intensity, the more difficult emotions can be to cope with.

Let's consider depression as an example. We all experience sadness at some point in our lives because we all deal with dissatisfaction and loss, but severe, high-intensity depression is a debilitating and dangerous emotion. It is natural and normal to become sad after a disappointment or a tragic event, but our general perceptions and thought patterns are typically not severely altered by it. We cope with the temporary sadness and then move on with our lives.

Depression is not so easy to overcome. It is a high-intensity emotion that can severely affect thoughts, feelings, and behaviors, sometimes without any identifiable trigger. Coping with sadness is a difficult but manageable chore while coping with depression is a long-term and complicated journey.

Destructive Emotion Is Suppressed or Repressed Emotion

"Our conscious mind thinks it's in control, but it isn't. Our subconscious mind doesn't think about anything, but is in control."
— Jen Sincero

The other common way an emotion becomes destructive is through suppression and repression. To refer to the popular adage, feelings should be expressed, not bottled up, or the pressure inside that bottle will continue to increase until the glass finally shatters. You may have noticed that I have included both "suppression" and "repression" in this section. Although these words are often used interchangeably in common speech, they refer to different types of "bottling up," and it's important to understand the difference between the two and how they affect emotional stability.

Suppression refers to the conscious, purposeful denial of thoughts, emotions, and impulses while repression refers to the subconscious denial of thoughts and emotions. Both are detrimental to emotional health, but it is repressed emotions that often cause the greatest amount of distress.

When you *suppress* a thought or a feeling, you are making a *conscious* effort not to dwell or act on that thought or feeling. The purpose of the suppression depends on what the impulse is and the situation in which it arose. You may suppress a thought because it is inappropriate or inconvenient to deal with at that moment. The bad news is, these suppressed feelings will keep manifesting, sometimes on an increasingly frequent basis, until they are confronted. The good news is, these emotions are often easier to cope with because they are something that you are consciously aware of. It's simple to fix a problem when you already know what it is.

Repression functions similarly, but these denials are subconscious, meaning you are not doing it purposely. Rather, your subconscious mind denies the existence of the thought, feeling, or impulse to such an extent that your conscious mind is not aware that it even exists. Repressed emotion can be much more difficult to cope with because it cannot be consciously confronted.

For example, *suppressed* anger may cause general irritability, but you can overcome this by confronting the anger, possibly by talking it out with someone you trust or by throwing some swings at a punching bag. *Repressed* anger, however, is more difficult to confront because although you may have rational suspicions, you are not consciously aware of it. You may only know that you are generally irritable but not understand why. You do not actually *feel* the anger that is harbored deep down inside you. Throughout this book, you will learn how to boost your awareness of what you are feeling and why, allowing you to begin to bring your repressed emotions to the surface.

Identifying Destructive Emotions

One way to identify whether an emotion is destructive or constructive is to consider how it is affecting the way you interact with your world: your friends, your family, your workplace, etc. Ask yourself some hard questions.

- Is this emotion negatively affecting my work performance or causing me to mistreat my coworkers?

- Is this emotion causing familial discord or tension among my friends?

- Is this emotion keeping me from doing what I want or need to do in my daily life, like pursue my goals or manage my home?

- What is the first thing I think and feel when I wake up in the morning?

The consequences of destructive emotions are all around you. You just need to be brave enough to look for them.

If you have a person in your life that you trust and who interacts with you on a regular basis, consider seeking insight from that person. He or she may be able to identify behavior patterns and habits that you haven't noticed in yourself. He or she may have noticed that a specific situation or person triggers your mood changes or that you tend to avoid certain things. The people around you can often be a great source of information because they can offer you different perspectives on your destructive emotions. Try not to take what these people say personally. It can be difficult to hear our loved ones describe our private emotional turmoil, but it can also be very enlightening.

Coping with destructive emotions is rarely simple and rarely easy. You can begin to identify your repressed emotions by listening to the body. When dealing with repressed emotions, especially anger and rage, the body is often as affected as the mind. Repressed anger can cause chronic pain as well as other emotional turmoil like high anxiety and depression.

Overall wellbeing isn't just about emotional and mental health—it's about physical health, as well. Your physical and psychological selves do not exist separately. They are constantly interacting with one another. Keep reading to discover how your poor emotional health may be negatively affecting your body and your physical wellbeing.

Chapter 3: Don't Let Poor Emotional Health Make You Sick

Your Body on Positive Emotion

"Our day-to-day positive emotions function as nutrients for our overall wellbeing. Today's positive emotions do not simply exemplify today's wellbeing, they also help to create next month's increases in wellbeing."
— *Barbara Fredrickson*

Scientists have been studying the positive effects of emotions for as long as they've been studying the negative effects, and it is generally found that people who experience more positive emotions tend to be healthier and live longer. When we feel more upbeat and positive, it causes our bodies to become better balanced, and our autonomic systems (especially the autonomic nervous system) function properly without the interference of stress hormones and other physical consequences of negative emotion. When we experience positive interactions with others and ourselves on a regular basis, we provide our body with a cycle of balance and health.

Your Body on Negative Emotion

"I have found that most people are more willing to accept physical pain and limitation rather than acknowledge and deal with the mental and/or emotional pain that might have caused it."
— Tobe Hanson

Sometimes, our emotional distress manifests as physical distress, causing negative changes in the body. If you've ever been so stressed out that you found yourself with your nose over a toilet or so angry that your vision begins to go black and blotchy at the corners, then you understand how intense emotions can make us feel physically ill. Perhaps, you've had chronic stomach pain for years, but no doctor has been able to tell you why because the cause is not physical but psychological. This could be because it is your emotions causing your pain and not a physical ailment.

A common physical symptom of poor emotional health is a change in appetite. Many people suffering from depression experience a loss of appetite and subsequent weight loss. The body still gets hungry because it needs fuel to function, but even favorite foods may become flavorless and unappetizing. Sugar, though, affects the brain's pleasure center, which craves the good feelings sugary foods cause. This may explain why people with depression sometimes gain weight and struggle with binge-eating.

Another common physical manifestation of intense negative emotion is digestive problems. The brain and the digestive tract communicate with each other all the time, which is why you may become nauseous when nervous. When you experience intense emotional distress, it causes disruptions in the natural contractions of your bowels. It also lowers immunity, which makes it easier for infection to take hold within the digestive tract.

Fight-or-Flight

Several emotions trigger the body's fight-or-flight response, including anger, stress, anxiety, and fear. The fight-or-flight response is a survival mechanism that causes rapid changes within the body that prepare the person for handling whatever situation triggered the response. This response is so immediate that it begins even before the brain has a chance to fully process the visual and/or audible stimuli.

The brain sends signals to the body, alerting the sympathetic nervous system that there is something wrong. In response, the adrenal glands flood the bloodstream with epinephrine (adrenalin), causing a series of simultaneous changes. The heart begins to beat faster to send blood into the muscles and vital organs, blood vessels constrict, blood pressure rises, and breathing rate increases. All these responses make the person more alert and sharpen his or her senses to provide the best chance of survival in the situation. When the brain continues to perceive the situation to be dangerous, it keeps the response activated through the release of cortisol, which has the ability to stop other body functions in order to provide energy for the emergency response.

Cortisol and epinephrine are natural hormones, but the repeated release of them can cause many physical symptoms. People who experience spikes in adrenalin on a regular basis are at a greater risk of having heart attacks or strokes because continual exposure to epinephrine can cause damage within the cardiovascular and circulatory systems (your heart, blood vessels, and arteries). Persistent exposure to cortisol is also damaging to the body. When the body's nonessential functions are shut down on a regular basis, they cannot function properly. Cortisol will pause function in the digestive and immune systems, causing stomach problems and increasing the risk of infection. Too much cortisol can also cause weight gain as it increases appetite in order to recharge the body following the fight-or-flight response.

Stress and anger are common intense emotions that cause the fight-or-flight response.

Negativity Bias

Why do negative emotions have such an impact on our emotional health? Well, human beings are impacted more intensely by negative emotions than by positive ones. This "negativity bias" is a survival mechanism meant to keep the person more aware of negative environmental and internal dangers so they can be dealt with first. Unfortunately, that means we tend to put three times more weight to negative emotions, causing us to ruminate on negative experiences while we let emotions like wonder, awe, and gratitude slip away almost as soon as we feel them. This is why what was generally a good, positive day can be ruined by one inconsequential negative experience.

Your Body on Stress

The word "stress" gets tossed around all the time, but what is it? When and why do we experience stress? Well, like any emotion, it varies from person to person. Generally, stress is the body's response to change (physical, environmental, or emotional) and affects not only the emotional self but also the physical self. When facing a major change, the body responds with the fight-or-flight response. The body prepares to act by boosting adrenalin and cortisol levels, increasing heart and breathing rates, and increasing blood pressure among other functions.

Stress is not a bad thing as it keeps you alert, helps you stay focused, and gives you the energy you need to face the constant shifts and changes in your world. Emotional and physical problems arise when stress becomes chronic or highly intense, causing the fight-or-flight response to repeat.

Your Body on Anger

I doubt I need to explain anger to you. If you've ever been cut off in traffic, felt mistreated, or had your patience tested to the full extent of its limits, then you've probably experienced anger. This emotion comes as a response to the perception of having been done wrong, betrayed, or otherwise hurt emotionally. When we feel an injustice has been done to us or to others, we get angry. Like stress, anger triggers the fight-or-flight response.

Anger itself is not always negative. It alerts us to something or someone in our life that is not right and motivates us to correct that and express our frustration. Incessant anger and rage, however, can be damaging to your physical health.

Chronic or mismanaged stress and/or anger can cause discomfort in the body and damage to personal health in a variety of ways. Here's a list of common physical symptoms caused by negative stress and anger:

- Accelerated heart rate

- Accelerated breathing rate

- Increased blood pressure

- General aches and pains

- Muscle tension and/or pain

- Jaw clenching/teeth grinding

- Stomach/digestive issues

- Lowered immune function

- Difficulty healing

- Dizziness and/or nausea

- Insomnia or trouble sleeping too much

- Loss of or increase in appetite

- Loss of sex drive

- Tinnitus/ringing in ears

- Eczema and other skin conditions

As you can likely glean from the variety of symptoms presented in this list, the effects of mismanaged emotions like stress and anger can vary greatly from person to person. Work through this list slowly and consider if you've been dealing with any of these physical symptoms but been unable to understand why. It's not always easy to discern the cause of discomfort in the body, but by realizing that physical distress can be caused by emotional distress, we can move forward with motivation to better our emotional health for the sake of our physical health.

Your Body on Depression

Stress and anger are not the only emotions that can cause you physical distress. Depression can wreak as much havoc with your physical health as it can on your emotional health, causing an array of symptoms and worsening existing conditions. Many people experience the physical symptoms of depression but may not realize that these symptoms have a psychological cause, which makes finding solutions to these physical issues much more difficult.

The physical indications of depression can be very similar to those caused by stress or anger, especially when paired with high anxiety. Many people battling depression experience muscle tension, chronic pain, digestive problems, sleep disturbance, and a loss of libido. Other physical symptoms are more specific to depression, such as chronic fatigue, which is a general sense of exhaustion. Depression can also exacerbate existing conditions like heart disease.

Many people suffering from depression in their middle-age may consider these physical issues to be a normal part of the aging process, and too often, so do their physicians. It is important to realize that these symptoms may not be an indicator of your age. Your chronic pain may be from years of blue-collar labor, but it may also be a symptom of intense negative emotion.

Your Body on Repressed Emotion

"Unexpressed emotions will never die. They are buried alive and will come forth later in uglier ways."
— Sigmund Freud

"But feelings can't be ignored, no matter how unjust or ungrateful they seem."
— Anne Frank

It is not only the emotions that we are aware of that can cause us physical damage. Remember, repressed emotions are not something you are fully aware of if you are aware of them at all. These are the emotions that we subconsciously avoid and ignore. Emotions are your body's way of motivating you to take action, so when they are repressed, the body suffers.

Your body expends energy in two ways: through physical exertion and through mental exertion. When emotions are repressed, the body is allocating much of its energy to the internal struggle with the emotion. This can leave you feeling exhausted when there is no physical reason for your body to be fatigued.

Repressed emotions are also a common cause of stress, which triggers the release of stress hormones like adrenalin and cortisol. As I've already explained, repeated exposure to these hormones can damage the body. Inflammation and muscle tension causes stomach pain, chest pain, and other aches and pains. Poor immune function is also caused by repressed emotions, making it easier for your body to contract illnesses like bronchitis, pneumonia, urinary tract infections, and other infections.

Listen To Your Body

Taking the time to consider what your body's physical health is telling you is an important step in overcoming your negative emotions. I know this can be difficult. Although I have struggled with anxiety and depression symptoms my whole life, it took me almost a year during the days that my depression was at its worse for me to realize that my physical unease was being caused by my emotional unease.

I went through a long period of time when I would awake every morning with the realization that I needed to throw up. This stomach upset didn't have much to do with my physical habits; it was my emotions that were making me so sick. My stomach was in constant knots, and I had to be very careful of what I ate to not upset it further. I was sleeping too, *a lot*, which further disintegrated my digestive health. It wasn't until I began to climb out from under my depression that I noticed my gut beginning to return to normal.

If your body is trying to tell you something, don't ignore it. It can be too easy to attribute physical discomfort to normal bodily changes, like aging, when, in fact, your physical symptoms may be caused by your emotional turmoil. It is also important to notice when pre-existing conditions worsen for no physically identifiable reason. Chronic stress and anxiety can wreak havoc on our bodies when we are coping with other illnesses.

Connect With Others

"Love is our true destiny. We do not find the meaning of life by ourselves alone — we find it with another."
— Thomas Merton

The professionals who study the physical impact of negative emotions have found that there is a direct link between perceived positive connections with others and improved physical health. The more we have good social interactions, the better we are at manifesting positive emotions within ourselves, and vice-versa, which relieves the body of a lot of physical stress. If we can maintain this "upward spiral dynamic" between positive emotion and positive social connection, we can more easily grow in our emotional selves and therefore improve our physical health. Here's a list of potential health benefits that can result from positive social connectivity:

- Improved longevity

- Stronger immune function

- Decreased inflammation

- Faster healing time

Human beings are generally social creatures, so it makes sense that we tend to be happier and healthier when we are making positive social connections. Be sure to make time in your busy life to spend time with the people you love and who bring your mood up.

Practice Relaxation

"During the time of stress, the "fight-or-flight" response is on and the self-repair mechanism is disabled. It is then when we say that the immunity of the body goes down and the body is exposed to the risk for disease. Meditation activates relaxation when the sympathetic nervous system is turned off and the parasympathetic nervous system is turned on, and natural healing starts."
— *Annie Wilson*

Another great way to counter the negative physical effects of intense negative emotion is through the practice of relaxation. When we actively relax, it allows for all the natural processes that can cause harm within the body (like fight-or-flight) to turn off or reset, providing relief from stress hormones, muscle tension, and other physical symptoms. The practice of meditation is an effective and therapeutic way to practice relaxation. I will discuss more benefits of meditation as well as a brief guide on how to meditate effectively in the next chapter. Keep reading to learn more about meditation and relaxation.

When we understand that our physical problems are linked to our emotional struggles, we can move productively forward in eliminating these destructive emotions and improving both physical and mental health. The first step in managing destructive emotions is learning how to identify our triggers and how we react to them. Once we understand our emotional responses, we can work to change them for the better. Are you ready to take charge of your emotions? Let's begin by learning how to recognize what triggers our intense negative emotions and how we are currently responding to them.

Chapter 4: Recognize Your Emotional Triggers and Responses

"In order to move on, you must understand why you felt what you did and why you no longer need to feel it."
— Mitch Albom

Feelings, especially intense feelings, can often be autonomous, which means they are automatic and subconscious, developing as the result of an external force or trigger. If someone cuts you off in traffic, for example, the anger that bubbles up in your gut is generated without conscious thought or intent. One second, you're singing along to a favorite tune, and the next, your face is flushed, your heart is pounding, and your teeth are grinding. You may even shout an unfriendly and colorful expletive at the offending vehicle, but why is this a trigger, and why did you react the way you did?

In order to take control of our emotional selves, we must learn to be aware of what our emotional triggers are and what our natural responses to those triggers are. The best way to do this is to practice mindfulness.

What Is Mindfulness?

"The present moment is the only time over which we have dominion."
— Thích Nhất Hạnh

Sometimes, intense negative emotion causes us to become disconnected or detached, moving through daily life without really engaging with our emotions and experiences. This feeling of being disconnected is very common in people struggling with depression and high anxiety or stress. In order to combat this emotional distress, we must learn to become more present within our lives, to live with our eyes open to what's going on around us and how that impacts our emotional wellbeing. To put things as simply as possible, we need to turn off "auto-pilot" and begin to be aware of how we feel and why.

As emotional beings, we are naturally mindful, but it can be difficult to be fully present in our lives when we are dealing with high anxiety or anger or other negative emotions. When we practice mindfulness, we force ourselves to face these emotions, to consider them and learn to understand them. We can cultivate mindfulness through a variety of techniques, the most common and widely practiced being meditation.

What Is Meditation?

"Altogether, the idea of meditation is not to create states of ecstasy or absorption, but to experience being."
— Chögyam Trungpa

Meditation is an excellent relaxation technique that also helps us connect with our inner truths. The goal of meditation is to quiet the mind and body, to remove insignificant thoughts, and develop inner balance by interacting with our emotional selves without the constant external and internal chatter. Meditation itself is a rather simple activity, but calming the body and mind is easier said than done. By introducing meditation into your regular routine, you will get better and better at it, and you will begin to crave the positive and peaceful feelings it can bring out.

How Does Meditation Promote Mindfulness?

When we meditate, we steer our awareness away from the external and turn it inwards, paying attention to what the body and mind are doing without the external noise of life. Meditation promotes relaxation, which relieves the body of stress and stress hormones and allows it to function more easily. When the body is less stressed, there are fewer physical distractions from what is going on in the mind. When we are meditating, we are naturally more aware of our thoughts and emotions, and we are open to the insights we have within ourselves.

How Do I Meditate?

When I first read about the possible benefits of meditation, I was hesitant to try it, mostly because, well, what if I was doing it wrong? It turns out, I didn't have anything to worry about, because there is no right or wrong way to meditate. It all depends on what works best for you and what is most comfortable. If you don't know where to begin, here's a step-by-step guide to getting started with meditation.

- **Set an intention for today's practice.** Your intention may simply be to practice meditation, especially at the beginning. As you become more accustomed to meditation, you may set a more specific intention before you begin, such as seeking intuition regarding a struggle in your life. If you choose to set a specific intention, begin with a question. How do I deal with ____? Ask yourself this question and see what answers you get.

- **Find a quiet, comfortable place to sit.** The most important thing is that you find a comfortable seat that is not going to strain your muscles. Cross your legs, or if this is not comfortable, spread them out in front of you so they can relax into the floor/couch/bed/comfy spot. If your hips do not like this position, try elevating your butt with a pillow or folded up towel. This can relieve tension in the hips.

- **Relax your body into an upright position.** You don't want to strain your muscles; allow your body to relax into the natural curvature of your spine. Relax your body from top to bottom, starting with the face. You can relax your face by focusing on relaxing your forehead and jaw muscles. Let your arms fall parallel to your body, and rest your hands on your legs. Work your way down until your body feels tension-free (or as tension-free as possible) and grounded into your seat.

- **Close your eyes or focus on a single point.** It is common to close one's eyes during meditation, but that can make it easier to fall asleep. If you do fall asleep, don't beat yourself up. It happens, especially when meditation is new. If you don't want to close your eyes, choose a spot in front of you to focus on. You may focus on a spot on the floor in front of you, light a candle, or set up a poster of a calming landscape.

- **Take calming breaths and notice your breathing.** It doesn't matter so much how you breathe as much as it matters that you pay attention to your breaths. Feel each inhale and exhale move through your body. Focusing on your breathing encourages mindfulness of the body and allows the mind the quiet.

- **As thoughts enter your mind, allow them to pass through.** When a thought comes up, you want to try to release it, let it flow out of your head as quickly as it flowed in. By emptying the mind, we allow our inner voice to be heard through intuitions. Your mind will probably wander, but that's okay. What you're trying to cultivate is an ability to be present at the moment and connect with yourself in a judgment-free environment.

- **Consider setting a timer.** Especially when you are first starting out with meditation, you will probably have limited stamina. Begin with short, five-minute sessions, working up from there to spend longer and longer periods of time meditating. By setting a timer, you can avoid the distraction of how many seconds or minutes have passed and instead focus on your practice.

- **Consider using a mantra.** When you think about mediation, do you imagine a monk sitting cross-legged uttering "om" over and over? This is called a mantra, and you may choose to use one if your thoughts are particularly lively. Choose a neutral or positive word or phrase and repeat it throughout the exercise. You may say your mantra aloud or in your mind.

Using Mindfulness to Recognize Your Emotional Triggers

For the most part, our intense negative emotions manifest automatically as the result of some internal or external trigger. This could be a negative thought, a traumatic event, or even just an unexpected change. What triggers emotions in you will not necessarily trigger others, and what triggers emotions in others may not do the same for you. This is where mindfulness comes in. When you find yourself caught by the tide of negative emotion, try to identify what exactly caused you to feel this way. Here's a list of some possible triggers for common negative emotions:

Stress

- Change in the environment (a big move, a new job, etc.)

- Change in family life (marriage, divorce, a new baby, etc.)

- Changes in social life (discord among friends, someone moving away, etc.)

- Change in health (new or worsening illness, an injury, etc.)

- Change or increase in financial responsibilities (losing a job, etc.)

- Change in the workplace (tension among coworkers, getting fired, etc.)

- General disorder (a cluttered home, child and/or pet messes, etc.)

Anger

- Betrayal by a trusted person or entity
- Being disrespected, challenged, or insulted
- Being physically or emotionally threatened
- Being patronized or condescended to
- Being lied to/given misinformation
- The injustice done to you or others
- Discrimination/prejudice

Fear

- Threat of death
- Threat of injury or pain

- Loss of perceived safety/security

- Dark or unfamiliar environment

- Imagining a threatening event

- Reliving past fear or trauma

- Feeling exposed/vulnerable

Anxiety

- Anticipating failure or discomfort

- Feeling unprepared or insecure

- Feeling inadequate or worthless

- Negative self-talk/self-deprecation

- Upcoming event, performance, or challenge

- Social and/or familial conflict

- Remembering bad experiences

- Personal strain (due to finances, travel, etc.)

Sadness/Grief

- Major illness in a friend or loved one

- The death of a friend or loved one

- Temporary separation from loved ones

- Feeling rejected or unwanted

- A loss of identity or self-worth

- Anticipating future tragedy

- Disappointment in self or others

- Involuntary memories of loss or disappointment

Once we know what is triggering our emotional distress, we can begin to put together techniques and strategies on how to cope with it in a healthy way.

Using Mindfulness to Recognize Your Emotional Responses

To gain mastery over your emotions, you will need to practice recognizing how you respond to your emotional triggers. If you're angry at your significant other because of something that was said, consider how you're responding as well as what made you angry in the first place. Do you shut down and avoid the conflict? Do you explode into screams and rants? Practice recognizing how your body and mind respond to intense emotions, and consider which reactions are positive and which are negative.

When you can identify what is causing your emotional turmoil and have the self-awareness to recognize your responses, you are better prepared to try coping strategies and allow them to work.

Coping with intense emotions is difficult when one does not understand what (s)he is feeling and why. Practice mindfulness to get to know your emotional self.

The Role of Self-Talk

"Positive self-talk is to emotional pain as pain pill is to physical pain."
- Edmond Mbiaka

One of the most important aspects of mindfulness is being aware of how you talk to yourself. You must learn to pay attention to how you interact with yourself within your private thoughts because poor self-talk exacerbates poor emotional health. Self-talk is habitual, and it can be easy to get in the habit of speaking to oneself from a place of judgment. We more readily notice our own shortcomings than we do our skills, talents, and successes, and when we focus our self-talk around these negative things, we influence how we feel in a negative way.

Consider how you talk to yourself. Do you tend to be supportive of yourself, or do you tend to ruminate on negative thoughts and bring yourself down? Here's a list of common ways people engage in negative self-talk:

- Self-defamation (I look fat, I am stupid, I can't do anything right, etc.)

- Self-criticism over a past event (I should've done, should've said, etc.)

- Doubting own abilities (the ever destructive "I can't")

- Dismissing own abilities and good qualities

- Focusing on own perceived faults and failures

- Personalizing things that are out of our control

- Thinking in black and white (in terms of extremes)

- Assuming we know what the future holds

By practicing mindfulness, we can acknowledge the destructive ways in which we communicate with ourselves to be more empathetic and forgiving of our emotional struggles. Once you get in the habit of practicing mindfulness, you can begin to build coping strategies to remove your emotional triggers and change your responses to the triggers you can't get rid of. You may even begin to do this naturally once you are more aware of your triggers and reactions.

Chapter 5: Remove Your Triggers and Change Your Responses

"You don't ever have to feel guilty about removing toxic people from your life. It's one thing if a person owns up to their behavior and makes an effort to change. But if a person disregards your feelings, ignores your boundaries, and continues to treat you in a harmful way, they need to go."
— Daniell Koepke

By identifying our emotional triggers, we can determine what is going on in our lives that causes emotional distress. While there are certain triggers that are just a part of life, some of the things that cause poor emotional health are removable. It's not always easy to remove a negative trigger, as it may be a close friend or family member, but sometimes, we must consider our own emotional well-being instead of the feelings of others. By hanging onto toxic habits and relationships, you may be preventing your own positive emotional progress. It could be a job, a significant other, or a friend that is causing you significant emotional distress.

How do I know when to let *something* go?

Whether it's a job, a substance, a responsibility, or another aspect of your life, you can determine when you need to remove an emotional trigger through a variety of considerations. Work your way through the list below and consider what's triggering your intense negative emotions. You may find that you are better off letting it go.

- **Get a new perspective.** Try viewing your job or whatever the trigger is through the eyes of an observer. What advice would you give this person? Does this person seem to be making positive changes or stuck in a negative cycle? If you struggle with removing your own biases, ask someone you're close to for advice. Ask what he or she would do in the same situation. Does this seem more productive than what you're currently doing? By gaining a new perspective on the situation, it is easier to see the problems and treat yourself with compassion rather than just suffering through.

- **Consider your joy.** You've likely heard it before, but if something in your life is causing you pain or stealing your joy, let it go. I'm not encouraging you to quit your job because it doesn't bring you joy because finding a joyful job is easier said than done. What I am encouraging is leaving a job that causes you significant emotional pain or makes it difficult for you to enjoy the other aspects of your life. When something is triggering intense negative emotion and preventing you from being happy, it's time to let it go.

- **Consider your energy.** Low energy levels are another good indicator of a trigger that needs to be removed. This may be as easy as building up a habit of going to bed on time, or it could mean eliminating an exhausting aspect of your life. Ask yourself, "Am I exhausted because I've been active and productive, or am I exhausted from the mental effects of something in my life? Is this aspect of my life worth the amount of energy I'm putting into it?" If it's not worth it, stop wasting your precious energy.

- **Write it down.** Get your emotions, frustrations, desires, disappoints, goals, and setbacks all on paper. By writing it down, you will force yourself to think critically about what is causing your negative emotions and whether this thing is removable. This will never be read by anyone except you, so be honest, and write what rings true to you. After you write, read it back, and notice patterns of negative behavior. Are you taking on undue stress by taking responsibility for something out of your control? Are there other negative patterns that you hadn't noticed before?

How do I know when to let some*one* go?

It can be difficult to come to terms with, but your most negative emotional trigger could be someone in your life, be a friend, a significant other or spouse, a family member, a mentor, or another important person.

Dealing with a destructive relationship can cause immense emotional turmoil. Sometimes, the best thing you can do for your emotional well-being is to remove this person from your life. This is not an easy thing to determine, so here are some signs that a person in your life needs to be let go:

- **You're sacrificing your beliefs and values.** It is important that the people you surround yourself with are supportive of who you are and what you're trying to do. They should lift you up and help you toward your goals, not steer you off your path with their own opinions. If you feel as if you are sacrificing who you are for the relationship that you're in, it's time to let go.

- **You feel inadequate or inferior.** It is difficult enough to maintain high self-esteem and self-worth without someone in your life who makes you feel bad about yourself. If you find that your significant other or someone else who is close to you makes you feel inadequate, as if you can do nothing right or are less significant without him or her, the relationship is negatively affecting your emotional health. You may need to have a long conversation with this person, or he or she may need to go.

- **You feel disrespected or unappreciated.** The people in your life should treat you with respect, thank you for your efforts, and express appreciation for having you in their lives. Relationships must be built atop a foundation of mutual respect, and it is emotionally toxic when this balance doesn't exist. Does someone in your life belittle you, dismiss your ideas, or generally underappreciate everything that you do? Distance from this person may significantly help your emotional health.

- **You can't trust or rely on the person.** When you can't trust or rely on someone in your life, what's the point of having him or her there at all? If someone you're close to repeatedly betrays your trust or is extraordinarily flaky, this may be a sign that you need to end this relationship. It's important for your mental health to surround yourself with people you trust and whom you can rely on.

- **You struggle to communicate or fight often.** Healthy relationships are built on effective communication. It's important that you can discuss things with a partner or friend, especially when something is bothering you. Is there someone in your life who you just can't talk to? Do the two of you have frequent arguments over misunderstands? Do you fight more often than you talk normally to one another? These are signs that this relationship is not based on good communication. If there is no chance of communicating better with this person, let him or her go.

- **The person never walks the walk.** Sometimes, people in our lives love to talk about the things they are going to accomplish or change or do or stop doing, but they never seem to make any effort. If there is someone in your life who "talks the talk" but never "walks the walk," it may signal that it's time to let go. This is especially true when it comes to your significant other. You need to be able to trust and rely on what he or she says. If you can't, this may be causing you significant emotional distress.

- **Your smiles are forced.** The people we surround ourselves with should make us smile. We should be happy to see them and happy to spend time with them. When you find yourself forcing a smile and a good time around a specific person, that person may not be offering you a healthy relationship. Ask yourself, "How do I feel when I see this person? Am I excited, or am I disappointed?"

- **You can't express yourself.** It's hard on your emotional health when the people around you don't acknowledge or value your opinions, feelings, ideas, etc. If you can't express your genuine self to someone you're close to, it may be time to let go. After all, isn't that the point of having family and friends?

Negative Emotional Responses That Hold You Back

"That which is denied cannot be healed."
— Brennan Manning

Not all emotional triggers are able to be removed from our lives. Some triggers will be inevitable, such as loss and work stress. These types of triggers are a part of life, so there is no letting them go. What we can do is find strategies to better cope with these triggers by changing how we respond. Intense emotions are not easy to master, and it is easy to fall into negative coping strategies, like denial and avoidance. Consider the negative emotional responses and coping techniques below to discover if you've fallen into any of these traps.

Denial

Denial is the refusal to accept the truth of a situation, and in short-term use, it is a healthy and effective coping mechanism. It allows the unconscious mind to deal with the situation before the conscious mind must deal with it. Persistent denial, however, can cause severe emotional distress; we all know that ignoring a problem will not solve it. Denial prevents us from dealing with our emotions and seeking support because we cannot face the issue at hand. It is so powerful, you may not even realize you are in denial until someone else helps you see it.

Avoidance

Avoidance is similar to denial, but it is much more conscious. It happens when we cope with certain events, emotions, or thoughts by avoiding them altogether. For example, a person experiencing high levels of work stress may simply stop showing up for work.

We avoid stressors in hopes of eliminating that stress, but this just causes more stress and more discomfort because we are not actually dealing with the emotional trigger.

Social Withdrawal

Many people experiencing emotional turmoil will withdraw from family and friends. This is not to be confused with simply needing some alone time, which we all need sometimes. Social withdrawal happens when we feel too exhausted, overwhelmed, or insecure to be around people whose company we once enjoyed. Human beings crave connection, but it is easy to fall into withdrawal, increasing negative emotions like loneliness and self-doubt.

Compulsive Behavior

Compulsive behavior is the repeated engagement in an activity despite sense and reason, usually to the point of obsession. We engage in this type of behavior because it can provide temporary relief against negative emotions like anxiety, stress, and grief, but it can exacerbate these problems by leaving us feeling out of control of our own behaviors. Examples of compulsive behavior include binge-eating, over-exercising, hoarding, gambling, and sex. For those struggling with Obsessive-Compulsive Disorder, these activities may seem very simple and insignificant, like hand-washing, checking (doors, gas taps, light switches, etc.), ordering/organizing, and counting.

Self-Destructive Behavior

Sometimes, we find relief from negative emotions through behaviors that are temporarily pleasurable but ultimately self-destructive. A great example of self-destructive behavior is smoking cigarettes despite knowing this habit can cause health problems later in life. We are often aware of the negative consequences of this kind of behavior, but we engage in it anyway for the relief it provides. Common self-destructive behaviors include smoking, alcohol abuse, drug abuse, binge-eating, and self-harm.

Catastrophizing

We can worsen existing stress by catastrophizing, which happens when we foresee the worst in a present or future situation. For example, the natural stress of a job interview can be intensified by negative predictions about how it's going to go. The catastrophizer may imagine saying something tactless and not getting the job, of never getting any job because wow, he or she is such a loser. Do you see the problem? When we expect to fail, we risk the creation of a self-fulling prophecy: you failed because you knew you would.

Changing Responses to Emotional Triggers

Having identified which of your coping mechanisms are holding you back from emotional balance, you can learn how to react more productively and positively. Practicing mindfulness will help you overcome your negative coping mechanisms, as will replacing these emotional responses with healthy, productive ones. Here are some tips for changing your negative responses:

Stop Resisting

Your gut reaction to intense negative emotion is probably to resist that emotion, but resistance doesn't help you work through it. To resist emotion is to deny, avoid, and suppress it, which prevents you from moving forward. You must learn how to control your emotional response rather than letting it control you. The first step in this is to stop resisting. When a negative emotion manifests inside you, face it. Directly acknowledge that it is there and why it is there.

Take the death of a loved one, for example. Facing the reality of your grief may be very difficult, but if you can acknowledge that yes, I am lost and in despair because I have lost a great friend/family member, you will be able to move beyond your grief. If you don't face your emotions, they will continue to bite at your heels until you trip, and they overtake you.

Analyze Your Response

When you turn to face your negative emotions, take the time to analyze them. Ask yourself, "Is this reaction appropriate to the scale of the situation? Does this emotional response offer me anything? What can I do to make this situation better? How can I learn from this situation to respond better in future situations?" Using your mindfulness practice is very important to this step. By getting to know our emotional selves better, we can better understand and change our emotional responses.

Practice Breath Control

There are several ways to encourage control over our emotional responses, but one of the best is learning breath control. When you breathe deeply and keep your attention on your breathing, you encourage your body to reset. This is not always easy, but it works. When breathing in slow and controlled, it encourages feelings of calm, but rapid and irregular breathing encourages emotional distress. This is why, when dealing with someone having a panic attack, the first thing you want to do is get him or her breathing normally.

When you are experiencing an intense negative emotion like anxiety, fear, or anger, take a deep breath, and try to take slow, controlled breaths while focusing your attention on your breathing. This act can help to lower blood pressure and slow an elevated heart rate. You may count the number of breaths you take if you're having trouble focusing.

Practicing breath control is an important part of many stress-relieving practices, such as yoga, tai chi, and meditation.

Be Positive or Neutral

One of the biggest aggravators of stress, anxiety, anger, and other intense negative emotions is negativity. When we come from a negative place, we fall into negative emotional responses that are ultimately unproductive. In other words, if all you do is complain about a situation, nothing will change. By focusing more on the positive aspects of a situation, you can address the negative aspects from a place of confidence instead of uncertainty. This takes practice, so you need to be patient with yourself, but over time, you can begin to stop your negative thoughts and replace them with positive thoughts.

Sometimes, there is no positive outlook on the situation. Sometimes, life just sucks. If you can't find a way to stay positive, try being neutral, even bored. For example, if you are dealing with a bully at your workplace, you don't have to find something positive about his or her rude or inappropriate remarks; there may be nothing to find. Instead, practice being bored by these remarks instead of letting them get to you. After all, words can only hurt you if you give them the power to do so.

Tips for Controlling Intense Emotion

Explosive emotions like rage, overwhelming emotions like grief, and paralyzing emotions like fear are not easily quelled. It can be difficult to think reasonably when one of these emotions takes hold. Here are some common emotions that cause a loss of control and techniques on how to cope with them.

Anger

If you are so angry that you can't see straight, let alone think straight, you may need to take a time out. Walk away from the person or situation that is making you so mad and have some time to yourself for a minute to practice breath control and regain control of your thoughts. Try to keep your muscles relaxed by keeping your fingers and jaw loose. If the situation is resolvable that moment, return to it once you have yourself under better control. If not, try to address it later when tempers are no longer high. Be sure not to ignore, avoid, or deny this person or situation as this can lead to suppressed and/or repressed anger.

For example, if you're having a fight with your significant other, it is okay to walk away. Let he or she know that you will be back, but you need to be alone to collect yourself, and go outside or into the next room. Avoidance is not the same thing as taking time out to get control of an emotional response.

Fear

Breath control is an important part of overcoming immobilizing fear as it promotes decreases in blood pressure, heart rate, and breath rate. If you have a fear or phobia that you want to overcome, try developing a curiosity for it and, if it makes sense, expose yourself to it repeatedly until it no longer scares you. We are naturally afraid of what is unfamiliar, so one of the best ways to conquer a fear is to become familiar with its cause.

For example, a good friend of mine used to have a phobia of bees. She had never been stung but had a very poor and embarrassing reaction every time a flying bug that remotely looked like a bee came near her. After she learned more about bees and their importance to the ecosystem, it was easier for her to not react when they were around. After repeated exposure to bees, she is now able to let one land on her without reacting.

Grief

It is important to grieve the loss of someone or something important in your life, but grief can snowball into a debilitating emotion if it isn't managed correctly. If you find yourself overwhelmed by grief, try to be more active. It is easy while grieving to withdraw socially and stop doing productive activities. Force yourself to engage with others and seek the emotional support that you need from the people you are close to. Don't let your life stagnate. Keep practicing mindfulness, exercising, eating right, and everything else that makes you feel good.

Understand that you don't have to feel guilty for moving on from a loss. Just because you have accepted the loss of that thing or person doesn't mean you've forgotten.

Anxiety

To overcome long-term anxiety, practice breath control and mindfulness in order to better understand and control your responses. When you find yourself overwhelmed by anxiety, try physical exercise, yoga, or even go for a walk. Getting your body moving can do wonders for calming racing thoughts and reducing levels of anxiety.

If you contend with anxiety attacks or panic attacks, use what you've learned about relaxation and breath control to calm yourself down during an attack. When I feel a panic attack developing, I find that a big glass of cold water forces me to slow down and breathe deeply.

Changing our emotional responses is an important aspect of mastering emotions, but you must also learn to recognize and eliminate bad habits and replace them with healthy habits.

Chapter 6: Replace Your Bad Habits with Healthy Habits

"Good habits are the key to all success. Bad habits are the unlocked door to failure."
— Augustine "Og" Mandino

In the last chapter, I touched briefly on the dangers of destructive behaviors, but there is much more to say. Our destructive habits, or bad habits, are the compulsive activities we engage in that may provide temporary relief from emotional distress but have the potential to be harmful to our physical or emotional health in the long run. Having these bad habits does not mean you are purposefully trying to cause yourself harm (unless you are engaging in self-mutilation). Creating habits is a normal reaction to emotional discomfort. The trick is replacing our bad habits with good ones.

Let Go of These Bad Habits

Here some common destructive habits that many people fall into to cope with emotional distress. Go through them and notice the ones that you use to find relief from negative emotions.

Poor Sleeping Habits

*"Finish each day before you begin the next, and interpose
a solid wall of sleep between the two."*
– Ralph Waldo Emerson

The relationship between emotional health and sleep quality is cyclic. Being overly stressed or worried can cause the sympathetic nervous system to be more active, making it difficult to fall asleep or remain asleep.

Inversely, not sleeping long enough can cause irritability, fatigue, sadness, stress, and other emotional distress. The body needs sleep to recharge and so does the mind. When we don't give ourselves enough time to get the quality sleep we need, our physical and emotional health suffers.

When lack of sleep is chronic, these emotional impacts intensify, perpetuating the cycle. This is also true of getting too much sleep. I'll go into more depth on this when we discuss hibernation. Consider how much sleep you get a night or if there is something negatively affecting your quality of sleep.

Poor Diet

"The food you eat can be either the safest and most powerful form of medicine or the slowest form of poison."
— Ann Wigmore

When we experience intense negative emotions, we may seek relief by eating overly sugary or fatty foods. These foods make us feel temporarily better, but they are detrimental to emotional health. A poor diet may lead to obesity and consequentially to poor self-esteem, it can cause us to feel fatigued, and it can cause confusion or "foggy" thoughts. Consider limiting your intake of caffeine and sugar, and see if that helps soothe your negative emotions.

You may not struggle with eating fresh, healthy ingredients, but other poor eating habits like skipping breakfast, binge-eating, or not drinking enough water can all contribute to poor emotional health. Consider your eating habits and how they may be affecting your emotions.

Poor Exercise Habits

"Take care of your body. It's the only place you have to live ink."
— Jim Rohn

Physical activity is important for emotional wellbeing for a variety of reasons. When we exercise, we encourage the release of positive hormones like endorphins.

We also become more confident because we feel strong and capable. Regular physical activity (even a walk) can reduce stress, anxiety, symptoms of depression, headaches and other muscle aches, and anger. Some of the emotional benefits of physical activity include improved mood, body-image, assertiveness, mental function, and immunity. Consider your own activity levels. Could you improve your emotional health by being more physically active?

Overworking

"Never get so busy making a living that you forget to make a life."
— Dolly Parton

Overworking can happen when you use work as an escape from your personal life or when you get so focused on work, you forget to live a little. Both forms are destructive to your emotional wellbeing. When we overwork, we experience burnout, which is exhaustion, detachment, and/or hopelessness caused by high levels of stress and pressure. This overexertion is damaging to your long term physical and emotional health.

Chronic overworking can increase the risk of diabetes, heart disease, and stroke, and it can exacerbate negative emotions like stress, anxiety, and depression. Consider your work-life balance. Are you spending too much time at work or feeling overexerted?

Hibernation

"I didn't want to wake up. I was having a much better time asleep. And that's really sad. It was almost like a reverse nightmare, like when you wake up from a night-mare you're so relieved. I woke up into a nightmare."
— *Ned Vizzini*

Oversleeping is not an easy habit to break, but it causes a lot of undue stress, it saps your energy, and it makes it more difficult to face the day. When you oversleep, you probably still feel tired because your mind feels foggy and your body feels sluggish. Regularly oversleeping worsens stress, anxiety, and depression, whereas, getting the proper amount of sleep makes these negative emotions decrease.

You may not hibernate, locking yourself in your bedroom, in order to sleep. Hibernation can also be an avoidance tactic when we are overwhelmed by intense negative emotion. Consider your sleeping habits and the amount of time you spend awake in bed. Are you sleeping so long that you wake up still feeling tired? Are you hibernating in your room to avoid a particular person or circumstance?

Alcohol and Substance Abuse

"As an alcoholic, you will violate your standards quicker than you can lower them."
— *Robin Williams*

Why we use substances like alcohol and illegal drugs to cope with intense negative emotion is not a secret—it makes us feel good when we're feeling miserable. That's why it's so common to see people self-medicating to overcome their struggles with stress, depression, anxiety, anger, etc. Unfortunately, alcohol and illicit drugs don't solve the problem. They only dull it down for a little while. Long term abuse of alcohol and/or drugs can worsen poor emotional health. I'm not saying you can never partake. I'm not your mom. However, consider why and how often you use alcohol or drugs. Below is a list of warning signs of substance abuse. Consider them and notice if anything rings true.

- You have vainly attempted to stop or cut back on drinking/using

- You are not honest with others about how much you use/drink

- Your drinking/usage has damaged or ended relationships

- You feel ashamed of your drinking/usage.

Self-Harm

"You might imagine that a person would resort to self-mutilation only under extremes of duress, but once I'd crossed that line the first time, taken that fateful step off the precipice, then almost any reason was a good enough reason, almost any provocation was provocation enough. Cutting was my all-purpose solution."
— Caroline Kettlewell

Self-harm can offer temporary relief from emotional turmoil and cultivate a temporary sense of control over one's life, but it does nothing to address the deeper emotional problem. Self-harm can take many forms, including cutting, burning, pricking one's fingers, hitting oneself, and even participating in unsafe sex. This habit is dangerous to emotional well-being because it is aimed at the self. Consider any habits of self-harm that you may use to cope and try replacing these with habits that help your body instead of harming it.

Develop Good Habits for Emotional Health

It's just as important to start developing good habits as it is to eliminate the bad ones. When we make time in our busy routines for positivity, self-care, activity, and connection, we encourage emotional stability and resilience. Consider the following good habits and how they may help you cope with your negative emotions.

Flex Your Positivity Muscle

One of the most effective ways to overcome negative emotion is to have a positive outlook on life. We become emotionally resilient when we can more readily accept and retain positive emotions and experiences. In short, when we focus on the good things, the bad things don't seem so catastrophic. I know, telling a sad or stressed person to be more positive is like trying to tell an enraged person to calm down, but this works, and there's good news; the more you practice positivity, the easier it will become.

Understand that being positive does not mean being perfect. It means accepting our shortcomings, learning from them, and moving on with optimism. Here's a list of tips and tricks for flexing your positivity muscle:

- Take time to wonder at nature and other natural beauty.

- Notice the good things you do for others and be proud of yourself.

- Connect more with the people you care about the most.

- Stop ruminating on your mistakes and misdeeds; forgive yourself.

- Let the past go, and don't let the future control you.

- Treat yourself with the same compassion you treat others with.

- Practice positive self-talk that is not self-defamatory.

- Accept constructive criticism and ignore the rest.

- Practice mindfulness and being present in the moment.

- Set measurable, attainable goals. Start small and celebrate every victory.

- Listen to music that makes you feel good/remember good times.

- Smile more. Even when you don't "feel" it, a smile can lift your spirits.

Practice Healthy Eating/Drinking Habits

It can be easy to consider your body and your mind as separate entities, but your physical and emotional health are tied together. The better you feel physically, the better you will feel emotionally, and vice versa. When we don't take proper care of our bodies by eating poorly and not drinking enough water, it negatively affects our emotional wellbeing. Be sure to take care of your body for optimal emotional health.

With so many diets and conflicting information out there, it can be difficult to know what eating right means. Put simply, you want to give your body good food that provides energy, vitamins, and other benefits while avoiding foods that make you feel bad. For example, you may opt to make a blueberry-kale smoothie rather than pick up a pint of ice cream. Here are some basic guidelines for eating right:

- **Do not avoid carbohydrates.** Your body prefers to burn carbs for energy. Instead of choosing white breads and refined sugars, opt for whole grains and starchy carbohydrates.
- **Do not avoid fats.** Your body can also burn fat for energy. Avoid trans fats and foods high in saturated fat. Some foods with healthy sources of fat include fish and nuts.

- **Eat more fruits and veggies.** Fruits and vegetables provide our bodies with essential vitamins and antioxidants. Try to choose a variety of colors, and don't neglect leafy greens, like spinach and kale.

- **Limit salt intake.** If you eat a lot of processed foods, you probably eat too much salt, which can cause high blood pressure and other health complications. Look for foods low in sodium and prepare fresh ingredients whenever possible.

- **Stop drinking your calories.** If you have a soda habit or drink a lot of sweetened teas, consider making water your preferred beverage. Your body needs water, and many people suffer dehydration simply because they do not drink enough of it. When water doesn't catch your fancy, opt for 100% fruit juice and other beverages with little to no added sugar.

- **Consider taking a daily multivitamin.** If you're not getting the proper amounts of vitamins, taking a multivitamin every day can make up for that. Vitamin D has especially powerful effects on energy, so you may notice not feeling so tired.

Choosing healthy foods and drinks is only half the battle of maintaining a healthy diet. Keep the following tips in mind to promote healthy eating habits:

- **Maintain a consistent eating schedule.** When we don't eat at regular intervals, it wreaks havoc on our metabolic processes. Try to eat at the same time every day to encourage a balanced metabolism.

- **Eat breakfast.** It really is the most important meal of the day because it provides your body with the energy it needs and kicks your metabolism into gear.
- **Eat slowly.** Too often, our busy lives force us to shove meals down at rapid rates, but this negatively affects digestion and may cause you to still feel hungry. Try chewing more slowly and savoring your meals to encourage digestive balance.
- **Snack less.** Try replacing salty or sweet snacks with fruits and vegetables or try drinking some water. It can be easy to mistake thirst for hunger, so if you find yourself feeling snacky, drink a glass of water, and see if that satiates it.
- **Limit late-night Eating.** This is not so much about the calories we burn while sleeping as it is about two other factors: (1) we tend to eat more when we have late-night snacks, and (2) we tend to snack when we're not hungry. If you feel snacky at night, ask yourself if you're hungry or just in the habit of snacking. Portion your late-night snacks to avoid overeating.

Another important aspect of taking care of your body is practicing good hygiene. When we're busy or feeling emotionally buried, it can be too easy to neglect the little things, like brushing your teeth, taking a shower, or doing laundry.

These things may seem insignificant, but neglecting them can cause physical illness as well as encourage feelings of low self-esteem, low energy, and stress. When we care for our bodies, we feel better about ourselves in general, and we promote physical health. Consider the following tips to maintain healthy hygiene habits.

- Clip and/or clean your nails on a regular basis.
- Wash your body with soap at least every other day.
- Wash your hair with soap at least twice per week.
- Brush your teeth twice per day, and floss once per day.
- Wash your hands:
  - after using the toilet.
  - after touching raw food.
  - after touching trash/garbage.
  - after sneezing or coughing into them.
  - after cleaning an open wound.
  - before eating.
- Talk to your doctor about sudden changes in your body.

Make Time for Yourself

One of the most important things you can add to your daily routine is time for yourself. It's difficult to cope with negative emotions when we don't give ourselves the time to be alone with our thoughts.

Alone time is essential to good emotional health because it helps us decompress, recharge, and feel prepared to face our daily struggles. Those who do not spend enough time by themselves tend to feel more overwhelmed or trapped by life.

It is common to feel guilty for taking time alone, especially for people with spouses, children, and other high-stakes responsibilities, because they feel as if they should be spending that time doing something productive, like housework. You should **never feel guilty for needing time alone**. Everyone needs and deserves time for themselves to practice mindfulness and self-care. If you simply don't have this time available in your busy schedule, seek help. It's okay to let Grandma take the kids for a few hours so you can refresh and recharge.

Get Moving

The role of physical activity in promoting emotional well-being is so important; I've dedicated an entire chapter to this discussion. Flip to **Chapter 11: Get Moving** to learn about how you can overcome your intense negative emotions through activity.

One of the most significant barriers we come across when trying to improve both physical and emotional health is stress, but we don't have to let stress run our lives.

Chapter 7: Don't Let Stress Run Your Life

"The greatest weapon against stress is our ability to choose one thought over another."
— William James

I have touched on stress a lot throughout this book so far, but I decided to give it its own chapter because it is such a constant and destructive presence in our lives. We experience both good and bad stress all the time, but the bad often becomes overwhelming, overshadowing the good. Once you understand what stress is and how to identify what is causing you the most stress, you can work towards finding strategies to combat your personal stressors and improve your overall emotional wellbeing.

What is Stress?

Stress is your body's response to a change, threat, demand, or even a negative thought. Have you ever heard the term "good stress?" This term seems counterintuitive, but stress can be a positive emotion when experienced at low intensities. It can motivate us to follow through on commitments we've made and goals we've set, and it can alert us to possibly dangerous situations. Stress becomes negative when it becomes chronic or highly intense and when we start to respond to it in negative ways. Negative stress can manifest as physical symptoms. Stress triggers the fight-or-flight response, causes muscle tension, and is therefore very hard on your body.

Here's a list of possible physical indications of negative stress:

- Muscle tension and/or pain

- Persistent headaches

- Skin irritation, like acne or eczema

- Poor sleep quality

- Weight fluctuation

- Digestive issues

- Reproductive issues

Chronic negative stress is also detrimental to your emotional health. Here's a list of possible emotional indications of negative stress:
- Irritability and/or agitation

- Difficulty managing thoughts

- Difficulty with memory

- Poor impulse control

- Feelings of worthlessness and/or loneliness

- Feelings of not being in control

- Unrelenting pessimism or worrying

- Feelings of being overwhelmed

Stress can be caused by a variety of events and situations, and I like to sort those stressors into three categories: Daily Stress, Change Stress, and Trauma Stress.

Daily Stress

Everyone experiences daily stress. We stress over our responsibilities, finances, significant others, children, friends, work, and physical health. National and global influences cause us stress, such as political and societal tension and media overload. Much of daily stress can be overcome by practicing positivity.

When we have a positive outlook on life, many daily stressors carry less weight. Mindfulness is also important in managing daily stress as it allows us to question why we are stressed and what we can do to relieve it.

Change Stress

We all become stressed when things in our lives change, especially if that change is unexpected or unwanted. Change can cause good stress, such as the stress of having a baby, moving into your first house, or starting a new job you're excited about, but if we perceive the change to be negative, it causes negative stress. We experience bad stress when we lose a job, get a divorce, lose a friend, or develop a serious illness. The key to conquering change stress is becoming more adaptive and resilient. We can do this by practicing mindfulness and relaxation.

Trauma Stress

The most intense type of stress that the typical person will deal with is stress caused by traumatic events, such as a major injury or accident, the death of a loved one, or a natural disaster. Coping with trauma stress takes time, but some of us get lost along the path to recovery, getting stuck in a cycle of negative emotions. To overcome trauma stress, we must face and accept reality before moving forward. It is key to take one day at a time.

Post-Traumatic Stress Disorder

Experiencing or witnessing a dangerous, terrifying, or shocking event, such as combat, assault, abuse, or other trauma can cause intense negative emotional impacts.

People suffering from Post-Traumatic Stress Disorder, or PTSD, experience the stress, fear, anger, and anxiety tied to that event long after it has passed. Flashbacks and/or nightmares may force the sufferer to relive the traumatic experience over and over again, often triggered by mundane things, such as a car backfiring, an unexpected touch, or anything that serves to remind him or her of the event. These symptoms may manifest directly after the event, or they may lay dormant for months before finally revealing themselves. PTSD is diagnosed when symptoms persist for longer than a few weeks, negatively affecting life at home, at work, and at social events. Here's a list of indications that someone may have PTSD:

- **Re-experiencing:** Sufferers of PTSD will experience at least one symptom of re-experiencing the event. This symptom is involuntary, forcing the person to relive the traumatic event through flashbacks or bad dreams. These intrusive memories may feel completely real to the sufferer as if he or she is actually reliving the trauma.
- **Hyperarousal:** For a PTSD diagnosis, the sufferer must experience at least two symptoms of hyperarousal, which includes changes in mood (increased irritability and agitation, hot temper, intense sadness, etc.), becoming easily scared, sleeping poorly, or trouble concentrating. Symptoms of hyperarousal are more constant than re-experiencing symptoms; these symptoms are not triggered so much as they create persistent emotional distress.
- **Hypervigilance:** A form of hyperarousal, hypervigilance occurs when the sufferer becomes overly aware of what is going on around him or her, always alert to possible dangers. Symptoms of hypervigilance include overreaction to perceived threats, exaggerating perceived threats, being startled easily, and experiencing the physical manifestations of fight-or-flight, such as increased heart and breathing rates and higher blood

pressure. Hypervigilance is a common PTSD symptom for combat veterans, who have been trained to be hypervigilant and struggle to turn it off in civilian life.

- **Avoidance:** Sufferers of PTSD will experience at least three symptoms of avoidance. They will tend to avoid situations, people, and other aspects of their lives that can trigger memories of the traumatic event. They also avoid talking and thinking about the event.

Short-Term Strategies to Battle Stress

Stress is so powerful, it can quickly become overwhelming. When the fight-or-flight response is triggered, your breathing and heart rate quicken, you begin to perspire, and your body is flooded with adrenalin. The emotional impacts of this bodily response can become too much. If you've ever experienced a panic attack or an anxiety attack, you know exactly what I'm talking about. If you struggle to overcome stress when it threatens to overwhelm you, consider the following short-term strategies for battling stress.

Counting/Waiting

When emotions like stress threaten to take control, one of the simplest things you can do is count to ten. I know, this is an old trick, but it forces you to slow down and think about the situation at hand rather than react impulsively based on intense emotion.

You may count silently or aloud, whatever works for you, or you may use another strategy to force yourself to wait. What you want to accomplish is to give yourself the chance to turn your mind away from the automatic response (be it anger, sadness, or another intense emotion) and toward a place of calm and reason.

Fresh Air

When the counting/waiting is not enough, take a break from the situation, and get some fresh air. Although there's something especially calming about a deep breath out outside air, this could be as simple as going into another room. Take a moment to calm yourself down and look at the situation from a calmer perspective. Whether it's an argument with your spouse or an unpleasant customer at work, sometimes, the best thing you can do is remove yourself for a short time. Just be sure not to leave and never come back. We must face our negative stressors in order to resolve them.

Pressure Points

Have you ever heard the term "acupressure?" It is a form of traditional Chinese medicine in which certain pressure points within the body are stimulated to relieve pain and illness. This technique may also help to calm you down in times when your anxiety or stress is most intense. Try activating the following pressure points while practicing deep breathing to help promote a sense of calm and relaxation.

- **Hall of impression point:** Have you ever been stressed or frustrated and placed your thumb or index finger to the spot between your eyebrows? This is a pressure point. To stimulate the hall of impression point, find a comfortable seat, close your eyes, and massage this spot in a circular motion. You want to use firm but gentle pressure. Doing this for up to ten minutes can decrease stress and anxiety.

- **Union valley point:** This pressure point is located on the web between your index finger and thumb, and stimulating it can decrease stress as well as relieve pain caused by tense muscles, like neck pain and headache pain. To stimulate this point, apply pressure to each side using the opposite hand's thumb and index finger, and massage it for a few seconds.

- **Heavenly gate point:** The heavenly gate point can reduce anxiety and stress, and it also relieves insomnia. You may need a mirror to find this point. It is located on your upper ear right by the triangularly-shaped depression. To stimulate this point, press it between your thumb and index finger, and massage in circles for a couple of minutes to relieve stress.

Diaphragmatic Breathing

We have touched on practicing breath control to relieve our intense negative emotions. It is a great tool for helping yourself calm down in a tense or overwhelming situation. Diaphragmatic breathing is a specific technique that helps you practice belly breathing, that is breathing into the belly instead of the chest. Here's a quick guide on how to practice diaphragmatic breathing:

- **Get comfortable.** Breathing from the diaphragm is easiest when lying on one's back. If you don't have anywhere to lie down, find a comfortable chair to sit in. You want your muscles to be relaxed. Focus on keeping your knees bent and your head supported. You want to allow your neck to fully relax. It can help to feel your diaphragm rise and fall, so you may place one hand on your chest. Place the other hand on your belly just under your ribcage.

- **Inhale through your nose into your belly.** We inhale through the nose during this exercise in order to take slow, deep breaths. As you inhale, focus on the expansion of your belly. Feel it push into the hand below your ribcage. Keep your breaths in your belly. The hand you have rested on your chest should not move more than very slightly throughout the whole exercise.

- **Exhale through your mouth, tensing your belly.** Purse your lips when you exhale, allowing your stomach muscles to tense as they push the air out. Feel your stomach fall inward with the hand resting just below your ribcage.

- **Stop this practice if you begin to feel lightheaded.** Remain lying or sitting down until you no longer feel lightheaded.

If you suffer from any kind of lung condition, especially asthma or COPD, speak with your doctor before practicing diaphragmatic breathing.

Long-Term Strategies to Battle Stress

Be Honest with Yourself

Many of life's stressors exist because we have unrealistic expectations of ourselves, other people, or situations. A common manifestation of this is perfectionism. To reduce your stress levels, it's important to be honest with yourself about the realities of life. For example, no one is perfect, and expecting perfection from yourself is a self-defeating cycle because you will never achieve perfection. Learn to accept your limitations and shortcomings rather than ignoring them. When you are honest with yourself and have realistic expectations, it is easier to progress, to grow, and to move forward.

The Four A's of Stress Management

The four A's of stress management are a group of coping strategies used by many to overcome stress. You may use one or all of these to help you deal with your high stress levels.

- **Avoid:** Although general avoidance will cause an increase in stress levels, you can use this tactic thoughtfully to cope with stress. You can practice avoiding stress by planning ahead, avoiding people who cause you undue stress, limiting your daily tasks to those you know you can complete that day, and learning how to say "no." Sometimes, we cause ourselves undue stress by accepting responsibility we don't have the time or energy to commit to. It's great to want to help others, but it's important to say no when this help is detrimental to your own emotional wellbeing.

- **Alter:** Sometimes, the thing that is causing stress is an alterable aspect of the situation. For example, if you're trying to get work done and a coworker is distracting you, assert your thoughts and feelings. Let that person know that he or she is being a distraction, and politely ask to continue the conversation another time. We can also alter stressful situations by finding compromises. You must also be willing to alter your own behavior if a situation calls for it. Find a compromise that is satisfactory for everyone in the situation.

- **Accept:** Acceptance is a powerful tool in stress management. When we choose to accept a situation, we eliminate resistance, which causes an increase in stress. When you make a mistake or find yourself in a situation you have no control over, learn to accept, learn, and move on. An easy way to practice acceptance is through positive self-talk. "I made a mistake, but it's okay. I have learned from this mistake, and I'm going to move on. I am capable. I will not be owned by my mistakes." When you find yourself ruminating on a mistake or other negative situation, remind yourself to stop giving these negative stressors power over you. When I catch myself ruminating over a past event, I like to use Jen Sincero's self-talk example from her book *You are a Badass: How to Stop Doubting Your Greatness and Start Living an Awesome Life*:

  "Holding on to my bad feelings about this is doing nothing but harming me, and everyone else, and preventing me from enjoying my life fully. I am an awesome person. I choose to enjoy my life. I choose to let this go."
  — Jen Sincero

- **Adapt:** There are several strategies we can use to adapt to our stressors. The first one I want to discuss is reframing the situation. When a situation causes you stress, try to look at it from a place of positivity instead of negativity. Changing your attitude towards the situation can remove its power over you. Often, we give our stressors too much power over us by losing track of the big picture. You may benefit from taking a step back. Look at the overall situation and ask yourself if it will matter in five minutes, five hours, five days, or five years. Chances are, it won't.

Practice Gratitude

"Don't take what you have for granted—celebrate it. Don't apologize for what you have. Be grateful for it and share your gratitude with others."
— Brené Brown

"Don't cry because it's over, smile because it happened."
— Dr. Seuss

When we're overly stressed, it can be easy to have a generally negative attitude towards life. We can overcome negativity and foster feelings of poise and appreciation through the practice of gratitude. When you cultivate an attitude of gratitude, it's easier to maintain a good mood, feelings of being satisfied with life, and overall emotional health. Here are some strategies for practicing gratitude:

- **Challenge negative thoughts with grateful ones.** When your thoughts turn negative and focus on what you don't like about a situation, try to challenge those thoughts to aspects of the situation that you do like. For example, when you're feeling stressed about a relationship and focusing on what is bothering you about that person, try to come up with a few things you like about that person. By reminding ourselves of the good things, we can take the power away from the bad.

- **When you're grateful for another person, say something.** Letting others know how much we appreciate them is a great way to practice gratitude. If you can, get specific. If your significant other prepared dinner to take something off your own to-do list, say, "Thank you for preparing dinner. Now, I have time to relax after a hard day." The more you get loud about your gratitude, the better you will get at recognizing the good things in your life.

- **Start a gratitude journal.** Sometimes, the easiest way to practice gratitude is to simply write down what you are grateful for. Try to journal on a regular basis at least once per day. If you can cultivate a habit for gratitude, you will eventually not need the reminders. You will simply look for the good things because that's what you always do.

Practice Forgiveness

Forgiveness is a form of acceptance, and it is paramount to maintaining emotional well-being. When we hold grudges against others and against ourselves, we allow the negative emotions to call the shots. By practicing forgiveness, we can take the power away from negative stressors by allowing ourselves to accept the past and let it go, which allows us to begin the healing process rather than remaining in a cycle of negativity. Professionals in the field have found that practicing forgiveness promotes a variety of benefits, both physical and emotional, including improved sleep quality, resulting in less fatigue, improved overall physical health, sometimes including the elimination of medication, and improved relationships.

If you find forgiveness a difficult practice, consider the fact that we do not forgive for the sake of others. We forgive for our own sakes in order to allow ourselves to accept undesirable situations and move forward.
For example, when we forgive ourselves for a past mistake, we stop that mistake from having power over us in the present. We are no longer allowing that stressor to affect our emotional health. To forgive is to let go of the past and commit to a more positive outlook.

Another great way to combat stress and other intense negative emotion is to bring more joy into your life. Keep reading to learn how to discover what brings you joy.

Chapter 8: Discover What Brings You Joy

"When you do things from your soul, you feel a river moving in you, a joy."
— Rumi

It may seem obvious that doing things that make you happy can help you master your emotions, but many of us neglect the things that bring us joy in our busy lives and suffer the emotional consequences. Many of us have been conditioned to feel guilty and selfish for taking time to honor ourselves as if we are somehow wasting time, but when you take the time to do things for yourself, you promote emotional well-being in a variety of ways. Having time for yourself is essential for mastering your emotions.

Taking time for joy promotes feelings of contentment and satisfaction with life, strong feelings of self-worth and high self-esteem, and increased resilience to both everyday stressors and sudden change.

"Me time" is as necessary for emotional health as a regular activity is necessary for physical health. When we neglect ourselves and stop caring about ourselves, we promote the increase of frustration, agitation, anger, anxiety, and social tension. If you find that you struggle with finding joy in everyday life, try some of the following strategies to add some "me time" to your routine.

Strategies for Cultivating Joy

Be Lazy Sometimes

Chronic laziness is not healthy, but neither is constantly being on the move. Your body and mind need the chance to decompress and recharge, so allow yourself some time to be lazy. Watch an episode of a television show you enjoy, watch a good movie, read a good book, play your favorite video game or game app on your phone, or listen to the kind of music that makes you feel content and happy. Not everything you do needs to be productive. Our emotional selves need time to relax just as much as our bodies do.

Go Outside

Do you find yourself spending all your time indoors? This could be contributing to your poor emotional health. It's important to get yourself outside once in a while and let your skin soak up some sun.

Vitamin D receptors can be found throughout your body, so when you're not getting enough of it, your body cannot function at optimal levels. Why is vitamin D so important to emotional well-being? It's the only vitamin that is converted within the body into a hormone, and this hormone is essential for the proper release of neurotransmitters like dopamine and serotonin, which are linked to a good mood. This is why we often feel more depressed during seasons of cloudy weather. The best source of vitamin D is the sun.

You can decrease your emotional distress simply by going outside and being in the sun a few times per week. Try to get outside before peak sun hours, between 10:00 a.m. and 3:00 p.m. Allow your skin to absorb up to fifteen minutes of natural, unprotected sunlight to soak up the vitamin D that you need. After this time, it's a good idea to apply sunscreen, especially onto your face and the tops of your ears. Professionals recommend 30-SPF or higher.

Get Creative

If you're an artsy person, get your paints out, sketch a still-life, write a poem or short story, or try a new art medium.

If you don't consider yourself a "creative," try picking up a new hobby, learning a foreign language, or starting a new project. The important thing is that this creative outlet is not something you *must* do. It shouldn't be related to the responsibilities you have or the commitments you've made. Find something that allows you an escape from daily life.

When we get creative, our anxiety and stress levels decrease because the activity helps us develop high self-esteem and promotes feelings of confidence and fulfillment. When we allow ourselves the opportunity to work through our stressors and traumas in a creative way, we feel more capable and independent, which elevates overall mood.

Be Social

All of us are social creatures, even those of us who consider ourselves loners or homebodies. Several studies have highlighted the positive emotional effects of having a supportive and loving network of friends and loved ones. Our lives are often so fast-paced, we forget to make time for the people we care about. When you neglect your relationships, the lack of connectivity causes increased anxiety and stress. You can promote a happier you simply by staying connected to the people in your life. Set a coffee date with a friend you haven't seen in a while, pop in on Mom and Dad, or spend some quality time with your spouse for a boost in emotional health.

Be with a Pet

Have you ever been feeling emotionally distressed and found relief by cuddling your cat or bear-hugging your dog? It is a fact that being with a pet can lower stress levels. Yes, having a pet can cause stress, but the overall benefits outweigh the negative stress that occurs when our pets get sick or won't stop getting into the trash. Professionals who have studied this effect have noticed that having animals around is a great way to reduce stress levels; cortisol levels decrease around animals, and having pets that need to be exercised requires us to do the same. Also, pets are cute, and being around cute things causes rapid brain activity in the parts of our brains associated with pleasure. Oh yes, there is a science as to why we get "good feels" when we see an adorable baby or pet.

Laugh More

"The most wasted of all days is one without laughter."
— Nicolas Chamfort

Laughter is one of the body's best natural medicines to combat stress, anxiety, and pain. When we laugh, our muscles tense, causing them to become more relaxed once we have finished laughing, which, in turn, causes a sense of peace and contentment. Laughter also causes the release of endorphins, promotes healthy function in the immune system and cardiovascular system, lessens feelings of anger, and reduces stress and anxiety levels. Seek out laughter in your life to improve your emotional health. You might see a comedy show, watch a funny movie, hang out with someone who makes you laugh, or find a way to produce humor in your social interactions. When you simply don't feel like laughing, you can still experience the emotional benefits by laughing anyway. Even a "fake" laugh can help you overcome emotional turmoil.

Using laughter as therapy may seem especially difficult if you are battling depression, a major injury, or a serious illness, but finding a way to bring laughter into your daily life will provide the energy and positivity you need to fight and heal. When we laugh more, we become more hopeful to feel more prepared to deal with all the ugly things life wants to throw at us.

Find Joy in Small Things

Sometimes, life gets so hectic and stressful, we forget about the little things that bring us joy. Try to take time out of every day to appreciate and find joy in small things. Practicing gratitude is a great tactic for this because it reminds us of these small things that we may take for granted.

Instead of stewing in negativity, find time to watch a sunset, enjoy a favorite meal, or play a board game with your children. The key here is to do things one at a time. When we eat meals in front of the television or play games on our phones while we're talking to friends and family, we distract ourselves from taking delight in everyday joys. Practice mindfulness to get better at living in the moment, and you will naturally begin to notice and find joy in the small things.

Pursue Your Passions

"Follow your own passion – not your parents', not your teachers'– yours."
— Robert Ballard

Perhaps the simplest but most difficult way to promote emotional wellbeing is to find satisfaction in what you do, and pursuing your passions is a great way to do that. When we actively engage in activities that we are passionate about, we promote the reduction of stress, anxiety, and general unhappiness. We find it easier to motivate ourselves to do the things we're passionate about, and we find gratification in learning new things related to our passions.

Understand that there is a fine line between following your passions and allowing your passions to dictate your overall sense of identity. Create realistic expectations for yourself and try not to tie your identity into your successes and failures. In other words, don't let yourself become bogged down when the pursuit of your passions takes you down a tough road. If you're a writer, for example, don't allow rejections to chip away at your self-esteem.

Try to roll with the proverbial punches and persevere. Don't push yourself so hard that you end up toppling over. Pace yourself, and remember why you're doing what you're doing. If you can't enjoy it, what's the point?

Chapter 9: Get Motivated

"If we are clear and committed, we will feel high levels of motivation. If we are unclear or uncommitted, motivation will be low. From this process comes a simple axiom:

The mother of motivation is choice.

— *Brendon Burchard*

One of the most difficult aspects of learning to master your emotions is getting motivated. Poor emotional health can cause a lack of motivation because life gets so overwhelming, and it also goes the other way around. When we have low motivation, we tend to be more stressed out, anxious, and depressed. If you have found yourself stuck in this type of self-defeating cycle, you can find relief by learning how to cultivate motivation.

You have most likely heard the adage, "You must make a choice to take a chance, or your life will never change." This is true in everything you do from mundane tasks like cleaning the house or finishing a class assignment to extraordinary tasks like finding a new job or career or packing up for a cross-country move. Action requires motivation.

So, what do we do when we can't seem to get motivated? Finding the motivation to do even the smallest of tasks in our lives can be easier said than done. Let's discuss some strategies you can use when you need a boost of motivation.

Strategies for Cultivating Motivation

Set Yourself Up for Success

Sometimes, our lazy habits are hindering our ability to cultivate motivation. When we stay in our pajamas all day, for example, we encourage feelings and thoughts of laziness and of not wanting to tackle that day's responsibilities and commitments. We can begin to counter these negative feelings by doing something as simple as getting dressed as soon as we wake up. Try to start your day with productivity, and you'll likely find that you are more motivated to take on all the things that need doing.

Set Measurable and Attainable Goals

One of the most significant roadblocks to being motivated is setting goals that can't be measured. When you are striving toward something, it's important to consider how you're going to measure your progress. If you can't keep track of how you're doing, how will you know when you've had a successful day? When we can't measure our progress, we lose motivation and stop making any progress at all.

Goals should also be attainable. When we set a goal we perceive to be impossible, it becomes harder to find motivation. If you're "reaching for the stars," try to pick the one you know you can grasp if only you can learn to jump high enough. I'm not saying don't challenge yourself, but choosing goals thoughtfully will help you find the motivation you need to succeed.

When you set a goal for yourself, set up a reward system. It's important to celebrate even the tiniest of victories, because feeling successful causes us to have more motivation. Focus on the benefits of completing a task or attaining a goal, not on the barriers between you and what you want. When we focus on the positives instead of on the challenges, we are more motivated to do the work instead of avoiding it until we have no choice or the goal is abandoned.

Practice Patience

A lack of patience can destroy motivation. Instead of focusing on the situation or task at hand, we focus on the frustrating aspects that cause us to lose patience. Consider a long commute to work.

A two- or three-hour drive to the office often causes impatience because, well, that's a long time to be stuck in traffic, but we can practice patience by putting aside those worried thoughts about being late or that annoyance at the doofus in front of us who clearly skipped driver's education. Instead of letting these negative aspects of the situation dictate how we feel, we can find a way to accept the situation and enjoy the commute. Maybe we'll listen to our favorite tunes or an interesting audiobook or podcast. If we're going to be stuck in the car for a few hours, we may as well enjoy our time.

Sometimes, it's the most common of tasks for which we lack motivation. One of the great killers of motivation is frustration. We can get frustrated when things don't go the way we expected them to or when we do not immediately see the results of our hard work. Chronic frustration stops us from being productive because it depletes our motivation and self-esteem. When we practice patience, on the other hand, we allow ourselves to pause, step back from the situation, and re-evaluate our current strategies. When something doesn't go according to plan, practicing patience will prevent frustration from negatively affecting your emotional well-being. Here are some methods you may try to practice patience:

- **Be mindful.** Practicing mindfulness is a great way to become more patient because it allows you to identify what situations cause you to lose patience and what you can do to change that pattern. If you struggle to identify what exactly is causing your frustration, try journaling or keeping a list of frustration triggers.

- **Take some deep breaths.** Patience can be cultivated by stopping to take some deep breaths. The key to patience is to pause, and deep breathing is a great way to take a moment to re-center before you must act or react. Try taking a couple of big diaphragmatic breaths when you notice frustration beginning to manifest.

- **Be Positive.** When we find ourselves in trying situations, the negative aspects can be much louder than the positive ones, but we can practice patience by keeping a positive outlook regardless of the frustrations. Practice "can do" self-talk, and challenge your negative thoughts. When your mind slips toward "Wow, this traffic is ridiculous. I can't believe I do this every morning," challenge that with, "Traffic is heavy today, but it's tolerable. I'm going to enjoy my drive."

- **Slow down.** This world moves at a rapid pace, and it can be too easy to get dragged into the hurry. Unfortunately, when we are always in a rush, nothing and no one ever seems to move fast enough. Find a chance to slow down and find some peace in your busy schedule. We cultivate patience when we pace ourselves. If the number of responsibilities you have simply doesn't allow for free time, consider if there is anything you're doing that either isn't important to you or could be delegated to someone else. Try to rank your responsibilities by importance and urgency to better manage your time.

THE EISENHOWER METHOD
Ranking Tasks by Importance & Urgency

1 IMPORTANT AND URGENT	2 IMPORTANT BUT NOT URGENT
3 URGENT BUT UNIMPORTANT	4 UNIMPORTANT AND NOT URGENT

Practice Perseverance

When we experience an intense negative emotion, it can be difficult to follow through, but we can reduce feelings of stress, anxiety, and depression by learning to persevere.

When we persistently pursue a goal, we feel as if we have a clearer sense of purpose. Perseverance also cultivates positivity and feelings of being adequate and capable.

Here are some tips for practicing perseverance:

- **Engage.** When we stop striving towards our goals, we tend to feel disengagement with life, which can cause our emotional well-being to stagnate. By practicing perseverance, we practice actively engaging with the present. Try to be more tenacious about life, and practice optimism and mindfulness to cultivate a sense of engagement.

- **Accept setbacks.** To persevere means to keep moving forward despite the setbacks you may face along the path to achieving your goals. When you are faced with a barrier to your success, don't turn away. Accept that something is holding you up, and analyze the situation to find the best way to proceed. The trick here is to not allow setbacks to cause us to give up.

- **Don't give up.** This one's pretty intuitive. After all, you can't give up and persevere at the same time, but sometimes, giving up seems like the best option because it offers immediate emotional relief. This relief is real, but it is also temporary, and the action of giving up ultimately produces more stress and anxiety. When you feel as if you want to just throw in the towel, consider the long-term emotional consequences and find a way to keep moving forward.

Conquer Procrastination

"Most answers reveal themselves through doing, not thinking."
— Jen Sincero

We all procrastinate to an extent, whether it's avoiding responsibility with the ever-effective "I'll do it later," proclamation or ignoring a medical symptom because that seems easier than possibly facing a major illness. As we've learned throughout this book, avoiding and ignoring our problems and commitments only serves to worsen our emotional distress. When we allow ourselves to procrastinate, we cause ourselves a lot of undue stress, anxiety, frustration, and low self-esteem. We can cultivate motivation by learning to overcome the urge to procrastinate. Here are some strategies for conquering procrastination:

- **Embrace the new and unknown.** We often procrastinate because we are starting something new or diving into the unknown, but we can stop letting these things affect our motivation by changing our perspective. It's common to feel inadequate or incompetent when we're first introduced to a new task or commitment. Understand that confusion is normal when something is new. Instead of allowing it to overwhelm you, try making your first step a brainstorm of strategies for taking on this new thing. Remember that it's okay to make mistakes, start over, or need help in figuring out how to do something for the first time.

- **Avoid task accumulation.** When we procrastinate, we have a tendency to allow our responsibilities and commitments to pile up on us, which causes increased feelings of being stressed and overwhelmed. Instead of waiting, complete a task as soon as it comes up. This is especially important for small daily tasks, like washing the dishes, doing laundry, or taking a shower. You may spend so much time avoiding the task that it could have already been completed.

- **Eliminate Distractions.** If you have a tendency to play on your phone when you're supposed to be working or doing something else productive, set your phone down across the room. This way, you can still hear it if someone needs to get ahold of you, but it no longer has the potential to distract you. When we remove distractions, it is easier to focus on the important and urgent tasks at hand.

- **Focus on doing.** One of the biggest procrastination pitfalls people fall into is waiting for motivation to strike. "I'll clean the house; I'm just not motivated to do it right now." If we wait for motivation to suddenly materialize out of nothing, we will never accomplish anything. Motivation doesn't just pop out from behind your couch and slap you in the forehead. You must cultivate motivation by doing. Action breeds motivation.

Seek Support

Sometimes, we need a little help in cultivating motivation. By sharing your goals with a friend, family member, or a professional, you can find the motivation you need to complete the task at hand. Having a support network is beneficial for motivation for a few reasons. First, it's more difficult to go back on a commitment or give up on a goal when we have shared it with anyone. Tell the people in your life what you are working toward, and let them help you stay accountable. Have them let you know when they notice you slipping backward.

Second, it is easier to get motivated to do something when you aren't doing it alone. If you're trying to start a habit of regular exercise, drag your spouse to the gym with you. When you wake up in the morning, you will know that he or she also needs to get up early so you both can make it to the gym before work, giving you the motivation to get up yourself.

Third, you can cultivate motivation in yourself by helping to motivate others. It can be too easy to get wrapped up in our own goals and responsibilities. We can often get stuck within our own worlds and overwhelmed by what we need to accomplish, but when we help our friends and family get motivated, we allow ourselves a break from our own frustrations and a boost in confidence and positivity.

Chapter 10: Get Loud

"In times of stress, the best thing we can do for each other is to listen with our ears and our hearts and to be assured that our questions are just as important as our answers."
— *Fred Rogers*

I've briefly touched on the negative effects of suppressing and repressing emotions, but it bares further discussion because it can play such a significant role in the intensification of negative emotions and the destruction of emotional health. Suppression and repression are what transform small irritations into anger and that pent-up anger into rage. They stoke our anxieties, inflate our fears, and bury us beneath heavy emotional seas like panic and depression.

The world can often encourage us to keep our emotions to ourselves. Many of us were raised on a "never let 'em see you cry" mentality that encouraged us to hold back our tears. For you, maybe it was "be a man" or "don't be a cry baby." We suppress and repress our emotions because we don't want to seem weak or incapable, we don't want to burden others with our "trivial feelings," or simply because we don't know how to express them because, well, we've never really done it before. We must stop keeping it all in if we ever hope to master our emotional selves. We must get loud.

To prevent the feelings that we've pushed deep down inside from spiraling into emotional whirlwinds, we must learn to express ourselves and allow these emotions to come out in cathartic, productive, and emotionally beneficial ways. I find the most relief when I express myself through two main avenues: journaling and finding someone to talk to.

Express Your Emotions by Writing

"Journal writing gives us insights into who we are, who we were, and who we can become."
— Sandra Marinella

Putting pen to paper gives your emotional self the opportunity to communicate with you in a language you speak fluently instead of trying to make sense of the emotional jumble in your head. When our emotions are all jammed up inside, it's difficult to identify feelings, understand what's causing them, and consider solutions without passing judgment on yourself. By writing down what you're thinking and feeling, you allow for a clear discourse between you and your emotions in a place completely free of judgment.

Benefits of Journaling

Maintaining a journaling practice is such a great way to express yourself because it can help with every aspect of your life from your work to your home. Journaling can help improve your emotional well-being by helping you lessen the impact of negative thoughts, notice and change destructive thought patterns, overcome habits like rumination and pessimism, identify repressed emotions, and improve mindfulness.

There are several other benefits to journaling, such as:

- Reduced levels of stress and anxiety

- Improved empathy and communication

- Higher self-esteem/more self-confidence

- Improved memory and cognitive function

- Improved problem-solving ability

- Improved restraint and willpower

- Improved quality of sleep

- Improved vocabulary

How to Journal Effectively

Although there really is no right or wrong way to journal, there are certain tips you can keep in mind to get the most out of this practice:

- **If it feels right, write.** When you're journaling, you don't need to write about any particular topic. Even if you're struggling with emotions tied to a specific event, you don't have to write about that situation unless you feel that it is right for you at the moment. Try to put words to the thoughts and feelings you are experiencing at the moment while you write. Write about your goals, your struggles, your failures and successes. The important thing is not to think too hard during your writing time. Just let the words flow out.

- **Keep your journal private.** You may find that the journaling practice will help you more when you don't share it with others. When we know our words will not be read by anyone else, we are more likely to be honest and non-judgmental. You may choose to share a certain insight or experience related to your journal with a therapist, spouse, or close friend, but keep the words themselves to yourself.

- **Maintain a routine.** The best journaling practice should be worked into your daily routine. Otherwise, it can be too easy to blow it off for other responsibilities. Designate a certain time every day that you will spend writing and try to be consistent. It's also important to figure out where you will write. Try to find somewhere comfortable to sit that is away from distractions, such as your phone, a television, or your kids.

- **Time yourself.** It can be difficult to write for any extended period, especially if you don't enjoy writing the way I do. It can be helpful to set a timer. This way, you can focus on writing without any need to look up and see what time it is. You should try to write for at least five minutes a day, but if you struggle with writing stamina, start with just one full minute, and then try a minute and a half the next day. Then, try two minutes the next day, and so on until you reach five minutes. Try to write for at least five minutes per day to get the most out of this practice. The longer you write, the more it will help.

- **Reflect on what you've written.** When the timer goes off, finish your thought/sentence, and then reread what you've written. At the bottom of the page (or in the margin), write down one or more things that you notice or realize while reading. If there isn't much to note from that day's entry, don't be discouraged. That's why we journal every day.

Free Writing

Free writing (also called stream of consciousness writing) may benefit you. You may opt to take on this freer form of writing in your journal, especially if things like grammar and mechanics slow you down by interrupting the flow of your thoughts.

When you free write, you simply write what comes to mind, whatever comes to mind and to just keep writing (not going back to fix things). If I think "Wow, this is dumb," that's what I write down. The idea is to get an unfiltered look at your thoughts and feelings without the added pressure of having to go back and double check the punctuation. You may even decide not to write with punctuation at all. A free write doesn't have to follow a logical path and probably won't. It will more likely meander around what you are thinking and feeling in an organic way. Reading back what you wrote may be a bit more of an adventure, but the results are unfailingly honest.

Express Your Emotions by Talking

"There is no shame in expressing your authentic feelings. Those who are at times described as being a 'hot mess' or having 'too many issues' are the very fabric of what keeps the dream alive for a more caring, humane world. Never be ashamed to let your tears shine a light in this world."
— Anthon St. Maarten

Expressing yourself is one of the most important things you can do to improve your emotional health. When we fail to express our feelings, it is more difficult to deal with them. Emotions that aren't addressed become repressed, causing negative emotions to intensify.

Defeat Emotional Detachment

When we suppress and deny our emotions, we run the risk of feeling detached from any emotion, even happiness. We don't allow ourselves to feel the negative emotions, like sadness, stress, anger, or fear, and the natural consequence is that positive emotions like joy and amusement lose their intensity, too. This feeling of apathy is a symptom of depression, but we can combat detachment by sharing what we're feeling. When we talk about our thoughts and feelings, we allow the opportunity to identify and cope with them. It may hurt, but allowing yourself to feel and express is what will help you overcome emotional distress and live a more purposeful and more present life.

Benefits of Talking About Your Emotions

Finding someone you trust to talk with to about your emotions is an important step in improving your emotional health. Here are some benefits of talking it out:

- **Gain a new perspective.** When you let someone else in on what's going on inside, you get a fresh perspective, a new way to look at the situation at hand. This new perspective may come from the person you are talking to if (s)he offers a good piece of advice, or it may come from inside yourself. When you talk out our feelings and thoughts with someone, you force yourself to articulate them, and you may hear something you didn't even realize you knew, or you may get a new idea on how to deal with the situation.

- **Gain clarity and insight.** When we fail to express our thoughts and feelings, they can often become confused and jumbled, but by talking with someone close to us, we are able to untangle the web. As I explained above, to say something aloud, you must first articulate it in your head, which allows you to make sense of thoughts and feelings which may have been confusing before. When you're forced to articulate something, you must identify and understand it, and that's exactly what we're trying to do.

- **Relieve the pressure.** Carrying repressed emotions around is not easy on your body or on your mind. Your muscles may be tight and painful, or you may clench your jaw or grind your teeth in your sleep. Your mind is clenching, too, in a sense, as it tries to sort through the confusing web of thoughts and feelings.

When we express these emotions, we relieve all of this pent-up tension and allow for catharsis, which is a re-lieving release of negative emotions followed by a new understanding of the situation.

- **Realize you are not alone.** One of the best things about talking about your feelings is you're likely to learn that your sibling, spouse, friend, or even thera-pist has gone through what you're going through. Eve-ryone's experience is different, but we all feel emotion. Even if the situation is not exactly like yours, take comfort in the knowledge that you are not the only one struggling. Not by a long shot.

- **Improve communication with others.** When we can more readily express our thoughts and emotions with the people around us, we will naturally communicate with them more productively. They will learn to under-stand you better, and you them.

Express Yourself to Loved Ones

Learning how to express your emotions to others through verbal communication is essential not only for emotional health but also for the health of your relationships. We've already discussed what happens when we keep our emo-tions bottled up inside, but what about keeping emotions from the people in your life?

Perhaps your spouse has an annoying habit, but you don't want to say anything because it may hurt his or her feelings or it may cause an argument. Here's my answer to that: say it anyway. He or she can't help to relieve your irritation without knowing what's irritating you in the first place. The key to working through possible tension in a relationship is honest communication, even when you're not sure what reaction you're going to get.

I'm not telling you to nag your spouse every time he or she does something mildly annoying. Sometimes, you need to wait to address an issue until an appropriate time, such as when your kids are not around. Just be sure to go back and confront the problem when it comes to things directly affecting your emotional health or your relationship with that person. If you're not angry anymore in five minutes, it wasn't worth bringing up, but if you've gone years simply tolerating behavior from a spouse, friend, or family member, speak up. Only by confronting a relationship issue can it be dealt with in a positive way.

Working through intense negative emotions isn't always easiest when talking to someone close to you. Sometimes, an objective outside perspective is what you really need to move forward.

Express Yourself to a Professional

Sometimes, the most beneficial expression of emotion is done with a therapist or another type of mental professional. By having an objective third party listen to your emotional struggles, you can often be more honest because you're not trying to protect anyone's feelings or their opinions of you.

A therapist can help you cope with stress, anxiety, anger, and the other negative emotions that plague your life without becoming a part of your life in the process, which allows that person to offer objective perspectives and advice. A therapist may notice a bad habit or behavior pattern that you were not able to identify on your own. He or she can provide support and an open ear in a place where there is no pressure to be or act a certain way.

A word of caution: It can be too easy to lie to a therapist, especially when you're first starting out with talk therapy. This instinct to tell half-truths and lies is a defense mechanism, but to get the most benefits from therapy, you must force yourself to be genuine and honest. If you catch yourself lying to your therapist, it's okay to say, "Sorry, that wasn't true. The truth is..."

Getting loud is an important aspect of mastering your emotions. Now, let's discuss the importance of getting moving.

Chapter 11: Get Moving

"Movement is a medicine for creating change in a person's physical, emotional, and mental states."
— Carol Welch

As I've noted already in this book, physical activity plays an important role in the promotion of good emotional health. You may practice several strategies to improve your emotional health but still feel fatigued or detached without the benefits of regular activity. When we exercise our bodies on a regular basis, we encourage increased vitality and feelings of strength, which increases our self-esteem and cultivates self-confidence. When we don't, our bodies are often stiff, sore, and sluggish, and that's sort of how our minds feel, too.

If you've never been all that active, start small and work your way slowly to whatever exercise goals you have. Start with a short walk once a day, even it's only to the mailbox. According to professionals, the long-term goal should be at least 30 minutes of physical activity every day. You may decide to park at the far end of the parking lot at work or the grocery store, or you may decide to simply walk up and down your staircase half a dozen times. Look for opportunities for activity as you go through your daily life. The small things add up over time.

Let's take a look at some physical and emotional benefits of adding regular physical activity to your daily routine.

Physical Benefits of Regular Exercise

- **Manage your weight.** Many people try to lose weight simply by eating less, but doing this slows down the body's metabolism and prevents weight loss. When the body goes into starvation mode, it wants to hold onto its stores of fat instead of burning them. By introducing regular physical activity into your daily routine, you can lose weight more effectively. When you exercise, you increase your metabolic rate rather than slowing it down.

- **Build strength and muscle.** Building up your muscle mass will not only improve your self-image but will also help prevent major injuries like broken bones by promoting an increase in bone and muscle density.

You will also feel stronger and more connected to your body.

- **Get relief from pain.** Your muscles need activity. Without it, they can become tense and tight, causing pain throughout the body. When you introduce regular activity into your routine, you allow your muscles to stretch and loosen, relieving pain and encouraging your muscles to relax more fully during times of rest.

- **Feel more energized.** If you often feel fatigued even though you haven't done anything strenuous that day, it could be a lack of activity. When the body gets regular physical activity, it functions more effectively and efficiently, and you feel better for it because you have more energy. You may also experience an improvement in your sleep quality when you exercise, which in turn, gives you more energy.

- **Reduce your risk of illness.** Regular exercise benefits your physical health in a variety of ways, which helps reduce your risk of developing a serious illness, like heart disease or diabetes. Regular activity lowers blood pressure, improves cardiovascular health, and promotes high insulin sensitivity, all of which allow your body to function better.

- **Improve your brain health.** When the body is functioning at optimal levels, so is the brain. Regular activity also helps to improve memory, making it easier to learn new things.

Emotional Benefits of Regular Exercise

- **Find relief from stress and anxiety.** Regular physical activity reduces levels of stress and anxiety. Besides the positive hormonal effects of exercise, it can also help you block negative thoughts and replace them with positive ones and help you feel more generally content.

- **Find relief from depression.** Professionals who have studied the positive effects of activity on mental illness have found that exercise is a great way to combat depression. One of the biggest pitfalls when someone is depressed is fatigue, and exercise can help increase energy levels, helping reduce depression symptoms.

- **Improve your self-esteem.** I don't know about you, but when I sit on my couch and eat half of my kitchen, I don't feel all that good about myself. After a good workout, though, I feel strong, capable, and confident. When you commit the time to give your body the activity it craves, you'll likely notice a big boost to your self-esteem.

- **Relax with ease.** One of the most common pieces of advice to improve emotional health is to relax, but this is not always easy. When the body's muscles are tense, it can be difficult to consciously get them to relax. When you engage in regular activity, you will experience a different kind of fatigue, the kind that allows you to sit back and relax.

Getting Active

"True enjoyment comes from activity of the mind and exercise of the body; the two are ever united."
— Wilhelm von Humboldt

Possibly the hardest part about getting regular physical activity is starting. You may have tried to exercise before but either didn't like going to the gym or didn't like the type of exercises that you were doing.

The good news is, going to the gym is not the only way to get active. Here are some different types of physical activity that don't require you to run on a treadmill, although if you enjoy that, by all means, run to your heart's content.

Avoid Driving

One of the easiest ways to get exercise is to avoid driving when you could walk or ride your bike. It seems these days that everyone's always in a hurry, but if you have the time for a leisurely walk or bike ride, take it. Even if this means you ride the bus three-quarters of the way to work and then walk the rest. Any sort of activity will help you make a positive change in your life. Once you are accustomed to being active, try riding a bike trail or going for a run. The ultimate goal is to try to get both low and high-intensity activity throughout each week. Avoiding driving may be a great way to get the exercise you need.

Try Yoga

If you're looking for something that will challenge you but is less likely to aggravate an old injury or pain, try a low-impact activity like yoga or tai chi. These sorts of activities rely on balance and body control and can be a great option if you have weak ankles or knees because there is no running involved.

My advice is to get online and find some free videos. You want to find an instructor whose voice you enjoy and who is easy to follow, even when you are not facing the screen. If you struggle at first with these types of exercises, don't worry. It can take a few sessions to learn how to engage the correct muscles to do the poses properly.

Hike a Trail

Another great way to get some activity is to go outside and enjoy nature. Find a hiking or walking trail near where you live and set a course. I find nature walks to be particularly rewarding because there is always wildlife to see. It is also much less tedious to hike a trail through the woods or in the mountains than it is to walk on a treadmill facing a mirror.

Play with Your Kids

If you have children, use getting active as an excuse to spend more time with them. Go play some tag, throw a ball around, or have a living room dance party. You might start taking family walks after dinner, march in place during television commercials, do yard work together, take a yoga class together, or add some fun activity to daily chores. There are tons of ways to stay active when you have kids full of energy to do it with.

A Guide to Building Your Exercise Routine

Your routine for daily activity is something you'll want to write down in order to commit and remember your commitment. Once you've decided what your routine will be, find a calendar, and write it in. While deciding how you will be active, consider the following guidelines to create an effective routine.

Choose Two Days to Rest

While you should be getting some sort of activity every day, it's important to give your body the chance to recover. Your muscles need a chance to repair themselves after strenuous activity, and you'll likely be sore, especially at first. Choose two days during the week to designate as rest days, and try to limit physical activity on those days to low-intensity exercise. You may do some low-intensity yoga, go for a leisurely swim, or take a long walk to stay active on your rest days. It's important to get some sort of activity to give your muscles the chance to move.

Remember to Choose a Variety of Activities

One of the most common pitfalls people fall into when introducing exercise to their routines is doing the same activity every day.

The goal is to keep your entire body active, so be sure to add a variety of workouts. For example, you might choose to focus on cardio and stamina one day by going for a jog and on upper-body strength on another day by doing core and arm exercises. Yoga is also a great way to get a full body workout. The important thing is that you're allowing each part of your body to get the activity it needs from your neck to your feet. Here's a list of muscle groups and a few examples of how to exercise them to get you started:

- Pectorals and Shoulders: You can work out your chest and shoulder muscles by doing pushups, dips, barbell bench presses, and overhead presses.

- Triceps: Your triceps are the muscles on the upper part of the back of your arms. Many of the exercises that work your pecs and shoulders also work out your triceps. You can also work them out by doing close-grip pushups and triceps curls.

- Biceps: Your biceps are the muscles in your upper arm, and you can work them out by doing bicep curls, barbell curls, pull-ups, and chin ups.

- Quadriceps: Your quads are the muscles on the fronts of your thighs, and you can work them out by doing lunges, squats, and wall sits.

- Hamstrings and Glutes: Your hamstrings are the muscles at the back of your thighs, and your glutes are your butt muscles. You can work these muscles out by doing step ups and deadlifts.

- Core: Your core muscles include your abdominals, obliques, and back muscles, and you can exercise these by doing planks, side planks, and crunches.

(If you're not sure what some of these or how to perform them correctly, ask a gym trainer, or find an instructional video online.)

Keep Track of Your Activity

Write down what you do every day in an activity log to track your progress and see how you're doing. If you don't keep a log, you may not notice how much progress you've actually made. You may also not be getting the results you want but not know why. By tracking our daily physical activity, we can more easily figure out what works for us and what doesn't. My only caution here is to NOT track your daily weight. Bodyweight fluctuates all the time, so these numbers will not provide an accurate measurement of your progress. If you want to weigh yourself, do it no more than once per week. Being active is about feeling better. Obsessing about weight will only hinder you and cause you undue stress.

Challenge Yourself but Know Your Limits

The more activity you get, the easier doing those exercises will become. It's important to keep expanding your goals and challenging yourself. Keep practicing that yoga pose that has been giving your trouble until you master it, and keep pushing yourself toward a healthier you.

The trick is not to go too big too fast. You must pace yourself and listen to your body. If you're still struggling to recover from your current routine or try to go too big and find that you cannot maintain proper form and focus, you are likely challenging yourself too early. Keep an eye on your activity log, track your progress, and use your best judgment to avoid injury. If you suspect you may be pushing yourself too hard, back off for a while.

Conclusion

Congratulations, you made it! Thank you for joining me through this discussion on coping with intense negative emotions. I hope you return to *Master Your Emotions* time and time again as you work to improve your emotional well-being. I have done my best to fill these pages with the best information and the most actionable strategies available based on everything I've learned through my personal emotional battles. It is not an easy task to tame the seas of emotional turmoil. This endeavor takes commitment and long-term hard work, but through these strategies, you can learn to master your emotions.

I have done my part to the best of my abilities, and now, dear reader, it is your turn. It is up to you to take your first steps toward a happier self. I wish you the best of luck and hope you'll carry this book with you through your journey. I have used these strategies on my own path to peace, and I hope they serve you well.

If you have encountered success through this book, please leave a review on Amazon and share your experience with me. Reviews are always much appreciated, but more so, I want to hear about your progress and the steps you've taken to master your emotions.

Lightning Source UK Ltd.
Milton Keynes UK
UKHW021844220221
379219UK00004B/642

9 781914 094637